A Place
to Walk

TITLE PAGE: The base of a red balloon on a blue ribbon among sparse drift picked up 8-15 September, Port Darlington, West Beach. Clockwise from the bottom of the drawing: yellow wooden golf tee, pastel-dyed plastic salmon eggs in a net bag, *Stagnicola catascopium* (Lake Stagnicola, old broken shell), *Stagnicola reflexa* (Striped Stagnicola, fresh shell of this large slender snail which we found only here), unexplained black plastic-like seedpod, Webberian ossicles (modified auditory vertebrae) of a Cyprinoid fish (Sucker or Minnow), *Alosa pseudoharengus* (Alewife, ventral scales and ribs), *Pleurocera acuta* (Flat-sided Horn Snail, old shell), *Stagnicola catascopium* (Lake Stagnicola, old shell), *Helisoma trivolvus* (Larger Eastern Ramshorn, small shell), *Dressensia polymorpha* (Zebra Mussel, fresh shell).

A Place to Walk

A Naturalist's Journal of the Lake Ontario Waterfront Trail

Aleta Karstad

with the assistance of
Frederick W. Schueler
& Lee Ann Locker

Natural Heritage / Natural History Inc.

A Place to Walk: A Naturalist's Journal of the Lake Ontario Waterfront Trail

Published by Natural Heritage / Natural History Inc., P.O. Box 95, Station "O", Toronto, Ontario M4A 2M8

Design: Robin Brass Studio
Printed and bound in Canada by Hignell Printing Limited, Winnipeg, Manitoba

Cipangopaludina chinensis A Chinese Mystery Snail from Grindstone Creek

Canadian Cataloguing in Publication Data

Karstad, Aleta, 1951–
    A place to walk : a naturalist's journal of the Lake Ontario Waterfront Trail

ISBN 1-896219-01-2

1. Waterfronts – Ontario – Toronto Region – Guidebooks. 2. Natural History – Ontario – Toronto Region – Guidebooks. 3. Trails – Ontario – Toronto Region – Guidebooks. I. Schueler, Frederick W., 1948–   . II. Title.

QH106.2.05K37 1995   508.713541
C95-931090-8

Natural Heritage / Natural History Inc. gratefully acknowledges the assistance of the Canada Council, the Ontario Arts Council, and the Government of Ontario through the Ministry of Citizenship, Tourism and Recreation.

Contents

1

The Lake and Us

Lake Ontario drains the land where 35% of Ontario's People live, but how well do we know it? Does it mean the blue or grey line at the end of someone's street, or a park where we occasionally picnic, or is it only the name of a pollution problem on the news, or an inconvenient barrier to driving south?

The emergence of the Waterfront Regeneration Trust (WRT) among the tangle of jurisdictions that govern the north shore of Lake Ontario may be a step in the process of learning to use land and water so that other species can go about their business as we go about ours.

Plans for a bicycling and hiking route of 325 km between Hamilton and Trenton have been sparked by the WRT, enlisting the cooperation of municipalities, to help People appreciate the shore of the lake as a linear whole, rather than as isolated recreational islands dotted among residences, industry and agriculture. In February 1994, my husband, Fred, was invited to a WRT workshop about reptiles and amphibians as monitors of environmental health, where the need for a survey was realised and the idea of having a naturalists' trail guide to the Waterfront Trail was mentioned.

In the spring of 1994 we began our survey of amphibians, reptiles, crayfish and molluscs for the WRT, and later with their support spent three months following the shoreline of Lake Ontario to describe, draw and paint what we found as rural-biased museum-based naturalists. As we were commissioned to treat the waterfront as wilderness, the reader may notice that we occasionally express astonishment at things that inhabitants of commercial urban habitats may regard as commonplace.

Until this year, we had spent little time on the lakeshore compared to the number of times we had passed it by on the way to somewhere else. It wasn't until we considered the project of hiking, biking and canoeing from Hamilton to Trenton along the north shore of Lake Ontario that we realized how spotty our knowledge of the lakeshore was. How good it would be to discover it as a whole and share the experience.

The west-to-east route north of Lake Ontario can be travelled at many different distances from the lake. Our preferred route has always been Hwy 7, through drumlin farmlands and patchy woods and swamps on the knobs of the Shield. Farther south and faster are the QEW and Hwy 401, the great arterial whizzways of Ontario. Trains run even closer to the lake, through the back yards of a random sample of habitats, while nearby Hwy 2 runs by the front yards of settlements and farms. Lakeshore roads run through farming communities, and suburban neighbourhoods, and are pleasant to hike or bicycle, often with the lake in sight.

Many beaches are walkable, though progress can be slow below bluffs or around soil slides and fallen trees. A route along the beach is at times barred by private property signs. Some deeds run well out into the lake, and many property lines that once ran along the shore have been eroded into lake-bottom. Although our route lay mostly where the bikes could go, we walked stretches of beach as often as we could. Beaches are ever-new, washed and re-worked by each storm and each spring.

We canoed down several streams, but only made a few excursions along the lakeshore. Landing places must be well known or researched beforehand, as the lake is large, and weather and water conditions change quickly.

The Expedition

Lee Ann Locker, a student of Environmental Studies at Waterloo University, joined us for the spring and summer. With our red Ford Ranger pickup truck, aluminum cargo canoe *Fairhaven Bay*, four bicycles, small Eccles travel trailer, Lee Ann and her small orange car, Fred and our eight-year-old daughter Jennie, we were a considerable party. Backed by a letter of introduction from the WRT, we moved as an exploring party through urban wastelands, city parks and nature preserves alike.

Certain segments of the trail were explored by Fred and Lee Ann while I was tied up with drawing and painting.

This has been a longer distance than my journal has ever covered on a single trip, resulting in a pile of hand-lettered pages 2 cm thick and a computer database of field notes that currently holds 2555 records of 576 species.

We navigated mostly with 1:50 000 National Series and 1:10 000 Ontario topographic maps, also consulting street maps and preliminary Waterfront Trail route maps. We did not go any place where entry was forbidden by signs, and never went where we would have to ask permission to enter.

While hiking, biking and canoeing. we collected mollusc and crayfish shells, plant specimens to press, and the insects that I drew and painted. This provided specialists with material by which to identify species or confirm our field identifications. During time spent in camp we were busy preparing specimens, studying maps and entering observations on the computer.

Shells, leaves, bones and seeds from drifted waverows tell stories by the handful, a quick and simple way of sampling the inhabitants of land and water. We dry drift on newspaper, store it in paper bags or cardboard boxes, sift it with compost sieves, and save it for further study. Even casual monitoring such as this is

Butterfly Weed

important, because the plant and animal communities in the Great Lakes are constantly changing through introductions and extinctions. Fluctuating populations may also reflect, or bring about, changes in environmental conditions that will affect other species too.

We have followed the convention of capitalizing the English names of species. When we say "Cedar" we mean *Thuja occidentalis*, Eastern White Cedar, "Poplar" means *Populus balsamifera* and "Cottonwood" *P. deltoides* (though the difference between these two species seems to be blurred by hybridization), and "Geese" means *Branta canadensis*, Canada Goose, while "Ash" and "Oak" refer to *Fraxinus spp.* and *Quercus spp.* respectively, and "Dogwood" is any shrub *Cornus*. CNR or CN is the Canadian National railway system, CPR or CP is Canadian Pacific, GO is the Government of Ontario commuter train system, the QEW is the Queen Elizabeth Way, and CWS the Canadian Wildlife Service. "Hydro" refers to any aspect of the distribution of electric power as a utility.

While our research was sponsored by the WRT, the opinions we express are our own. When we refer to the Waterfront Trail route, this is the preliminary route shown on the maps we had, which differed in places from the eventual route designated for heavy public use and described in the WRT's guidebook, *The Waterfront Trail*. Some big stretches that we couldn't enter (such as Darlington Nuclear Generating Station) are now open as part of the Waterfront Trail route.

Before the Waterfront Trail was opened in the spring of 1995, we explored it as we do any wild area. Every twig and shell we picked up became a museum specimen. We do not encourage the taking of specimens for private collections or any use of land or vegetation that causes obvious damage. If everyone goes off-trail as frequently as we have, No Trespassing signs may follow. Stay on the trail.

We refer here and there to eating berries and other wild foods. Do not attempt to emulate us unless you too are well versed in wild foods and your identifications are reliable, and never over-harvest. Wild berries on private property belong to the property owner.

Parks, harbour and conservation authorities, and private people graciously gave us permission to camp at each site, usually for a stay of five to ten days. Each chapter describes the places we visited from one of our camps, though some episodes have been wrenched out of chronological into more nearly geographic order. You may have seen our little white trailer, attended by bicycles, plant press and coolers, as you walked your Dog in a park during the summer of 1994 and wondered what we were doing. This book is for you, for those who helped and encouraged us, and for everyone who loves the lakeshore.

This book is also an invitation to come after us and continue our work of surveying the snails, crayfish, and amphibians and reptiles of the north shore of Lake Ontario, in hope of a future of health and regeneration.

2

Auditory Station Spring

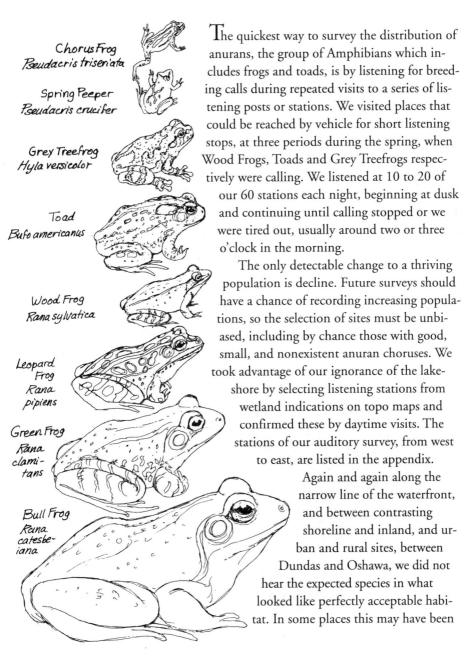

Chorus Frog
Pseudacris triseriata

Spring Peeper
Pseudacris crucifer

Grey Treefrog
Hyla versicolor

Toad
Bufo americanus

Wood Frog
Rana sylvatica

Leopard
Frog
*Rana
pipiens*

Green Frog
*Rana
clami-
tans*

Bull Frog
*Rana
catesbe-
iana*

The quickest way to survey the distribution of anurans, the group of Amphibians which includes frogs and toads, is by listening for breeding calls during repeated visits to a series of listening posts or stations. We visited places that could be reached by vehicle for short listening stops, at three periods during the spring, when Wood Frogs, Toads and Grey Treefrogs respectively were calling. We listened at 10 to 20 of our 60 stations each night, beginning at dusk and continuing until calling stopped or we were tired out, usually around two or three o'clock in the morning.

The only detectable change to a thriving population is decline. Future surveys should have a chance of recording increasing populations, so the selection of sites must be unbiased, including by chance those with good, small, and nonexistent anuran choruses. We took advantage of our ignorance of the lakeshore by selecting listening stations from wetland indications on topo maps and confirmed these by daytime visits. The stations of our auditory survey, from west to east, are listed in the appendix.

Again and again along the narrow line of the waterfront, and between contrasting shoreline and inland, and urban and rural sites, between Dundas and Oshawa, we did not hear the expected species in what looked like perfectly acceptable habitat. In some places this may have been because of some damage to the habitat that was not evident to us. In other places, migration or dispersal routes for amphibians may have been cut off. Fluctuations of lake level, and the presence of fish and other predators, need only prevent successful breeding for a couple of years to drive a population to extinction if new colonists cannot move between isolated beach ponds or creek-mouth marshes. Amphibians are sensitive to so many environmental influences that their naturally fluctuating population levels are not reliable indicators of habitat degradation. But their extirpation from a broad area is certainly a signal that serious damage has been done.

Spring often seems to stall sometime between snow melt and frog call. On 30 March we drove east out of Toronto to look for auditory survey sites. It was still 6.5°C at 14:40 on our first visit to the lake just west of the Pickering Nuclear Generating Station.

We parked at the end of a road al-

lowance, near a wide muddy track west into the Ontario Hydro property. Below us we saw a steep gravel bluff eroded onto the narrow beach, where an ice-push ridge was cut by seepage streams. Two advanced buds of Coltsfoot, in crumbly loose soil just below the brink of the bluff, were our first spring flowers. This European wildflower dominates the bluff-face vegetation all along Lake Ontario. It sends up its dandelion-like yellow flowers on scaly stalks in early spring, and its broad green leaves come out only after the seeds are fluffed away. Our first dead gull, a dusky-plumaged juvenile Ringbill on the brink of the bluff, is equally characteristic of the lakeshore.

Arriving at Squires Beach, we noticed plenty of activity at birdfeeders, where recent spring arrivals, Redwings, Grackles, and Mourning Doves took turns with Chickadees and black Squirrels. We visited the parking place by the mouth of Duffins Creek in the early 1970s with our friend Frank Ross, who taught me how to keep a nature journal. Duffins Creek is also the site of the first published report of the aggressive introduced crayfish *Orconectes rusticus* in southern Ontario, and we wondered if we would find it there now.

A path along the bluff edge of a grassy field led us to the creek

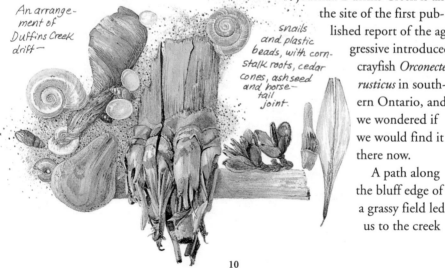

An arrangement of Duffins Creek drift —

snails and plastic beads, with cornstalk roots, cedar cones, ashseed and horsetail joint.

10

mouth, which was thronged by Canada Geese. They approached us watchfully, standing in the shallows to wait for handouts. Jennie lured them closer with a handful of pebbles. Drift along the beach was being lifted and pushed by the waves. There were such masses of land and aquatic snails in the little bay just to the west of the creek mouth that we could can hardly step anywhere without crushing shells. There were no Zebra Mussels, and the one crayfish claw appeared to be an ordinary *O. virilis*, not the litter of shelly parts characteristic of invasive populations of *O. rusticus*. Among the drift we found a Coconut. We presumed it did not represent a reproducing population, and breaking it open we found its flesh firm and sweet.

The old dead Elm in the high sandy field west of the creek was being cut up for firewood. I remember Frank striking its branches as a many-toned drum. Right on the tip of the point stands a grove of mature Sugar and Silver Maple, Willow, Ash, Basswood and Horse Chestnut trees. An historical plaque at the mossy old family cemetery of the homesteaders calls this Simcoe Point. Apparently this land was first commercially farmed by the Peak family. The row of old White Spruce marks the laneway of their house, and the old Apple trees survive from the Simcoe homestead.

In Oshawa, Stone Street ends at a long sand bar between Pumphouse Marsh and the pebbles of the gravel beach. We walked along the bar and farther east along the beach. Among brush and Poplars on the bar, we noticed white scraps of eggshell around six predator-opened turtle nests. Most of the carefully excavated, laid and covered nests of Painted and Snapping Turtles escape detection by Raccoons and Skunks only if rain washes the female's scent away. At the east end of the bar the outlet of Pumphouse Marsh was newly dammed and channelled onto the grounds of the Oshawa Water Supply Plant. The plant's trickling outflow smelled of chlorine as we crossed it on the beach.

The defenders of a few cottage-like houses had piled brush and rocks on the shore to try to retard the erosion of their foundations, and I smelled sewage seeping below one of them. Beyond this the steep clay bluff is actively slumping, and the shore is mirey with clay. Mats of felty algae bestrewed a beach of lovely rounded stones. Fred picked up the impressively toothy jaws of a Salmon, but there was no shelly drift to be seen.

Oshawa Harbour is the deep, curved mouth of Oshawa Creek. A large red and white Coast Guard boat lay moored beside a navigation tower. Three grey salt domes, oil storage tanks, and blue elevator derrick dominated the opposite bank, with a yellow-grassed dune and the lake beyond. Fred sampled a sparse drift of minute shells from the recreational sand beach beside the breakwater on the west shore. We started home at dusk, disappointed that it was too cold to begin our auditory survey. It was 11 April before we heard any calling frogs at home.

On Queens Quay West, Toronto, the 15th of April was a hazy warm spring day in the rushing city. Moving cars flashed points and barbs of sunlight. Glass-walled skyscrapers reflected themselves mirroring the sky in each other's windows and

Whitethroat Sparrow *Zonotrichia albicolis*

threw the roar of traffic back and forth across the windy canyon of the street. Everything was rushing. Beyond parking lots the Gardiner Expressway rushed like an elevated river of rubber, steel, paint, and glass, and behind the tall buildings the wind rushed over the choppy chalk-green harbour.

One thing had stopped. A Whitethroat Sparrow was too abruptly deflected by a sky-reflecting tower, its northward migration cut short. It lay limp, warm and fluffy on the concrete where we walked in the shadow of walls of glass. A pair of Mallards loitered about the concrete sea wall as we emerged from the Harbourfront Terminal. Gulls and Pigeons seemed as plentiful as ever, but waterfowl, except for this pair of ducks, had left their winter havens to reclaim spring territories.

We joined the early Friday afternoon rush hour traffic on our way to Whitby to establish as many of Fred's auditory stations as possible before dark. I rested in the front seat of the truck, appalled by the briskness of the wind at Port Whitby, while Fred collected drift beneath water-edge Wil-

lows and Jennie coaxed and chased Canada Geese. There were 83 cropping the sprouting lawn grass by the bridge, and two pairs of Mute Swans in the harbour, cruising grandly with all sails set. One swan cob came up on the road with the geese, and Jennie drew him in her journal as he terrified small girls into giving him the largest portions of bread and doughnuts.

On the road into Second Marsh we passed many People fishing in Harmony Creek, and found our way past the big shiny General Motors building to the road's end near the head of McLaughlin Bay. I made supper on the tailgate of the truck as Fred followed trails to the Second Marsh outlet, where he found a stream coming through a barrier beach. Fishermen were clustered at the stream mouth, and one was leaving with a silvery Salmonid. Behind the bar the lake had flooded into a mucky Willow-tree backwater, and Fred gathered a little drift from the limit of the flooding. There were only a few snails, among Cattail leaves and *Scirpus* rootstocks.

Second Marsh and McLaughlin Bay are maintained as a wildlife refuge by General Motors, which occupies an imposing new office building on the knoll between them. The only forest is tall wetland Willows, tousled in picturesque angles, and the uplands are open tall-grass fields, with a variety of nursery shrubs and little trees planted among them inside plastic collars.

Fred walked along the beach to the southwest end of McLaughlin Bay, and in the corner of marsh behind the barrier beach he picked up sparse newly deposited wind-driven drift very barren of shells. There is a platform for an Eagle nest there, and he found the leg bones and body feathers of a Great Blue Heron below it. One can't estimate low populations of snails from a lack of drifted shells, but it certainly looks like an indication of the historic pollution of these marshes.

We decided to make the head of McLaughlin Bay one of our auditory stations. At nightfall the air was 13°C. We stood quiet, our mouths open slightly to help us catch the faintest sounds, and listened for 10 minutes. Geese were honking, and two Woodcock "peented" on the ground and then flew, twittering, despite terrific highway and train noise, but no frogs called. Then as we climbed into the truck, we heard Coyotes in short choruses, but still no frogs.

At the Harmony Creek bridge, a marshy creek with a Willow-tree swamp and a sewage plant, we heard only a few Wood Frogs from the grassy marsh. Such a habitat, at that date and temperature, should be ringing with Peepers, creaking with Chorus Frogs, quacking with Wood Frogs, and snoring with Leopard Frogs. We visited 10 stations that night, only hearing Wood Frogs at three of them, and finishing just short of midnight at Squires

Beach. This set the pattern that we found all along in our auditory survey: no hylids (Peepers, Chorus Frogs or Greytree Frogs) heard in urban and suburban areas, and only small populations of Rana (Leopard, Green and Bull Frogs).

A strong tailwind followed us the next day, as we travelled east from Squires Beach to Trenton. In Trenton we looked for shelter from the wind so that we could repack the truck. We found two interesting concrete ruins that I hope to paint someday, a pair of rectangular structures that looked as if they might have been blast furnaces, and, in a hillside forest, a long concrete footing scalloped along its top edge, as if it had been a support for a battery of water pipes. We found our shelter in the lee of a steep isolated hill, The Mountain, in the yard of the Trenton Public Utilities building. I repacked and cooked pots of food to wrap in towels to take with us while Fred searched the wooded hillside for snails and salamanders, and Jennie played on swings. Then, turning into the wind, we began to locate the eastern listening stations, happily hearing afternoon Chorus Frogs and Spring Peepers along the Murray Canal, but it was too cold and windy to listen at night.

I spent the morning of 17 April in the front seat of the truck, drawing the view from the crest of the old Lake Iroquois shore terrace, 2 km north of Colborne, near a radio tower and large water tank in a pasture, with ploughed and stubble fields all about. We woke

to

sunshine, though
the wind had not abated. The truck
nosed into the lee of a row of Cherry
trees, Maples, White Oaks and a furze
of Sumacs at the brink of the steep
grassy slope. Far below, Hwy 401 was
in constant motion, roaring faintly as
tiny cars and trucks slide along its double strand. Bright across the wide water
in the distance was the thin blue edge
of Prince Edward County, and just before the shore, in rich dark purple, is
the distance-flattened hook shape of
Presqu'ile Provincial Park and, off its
tip, High Bluff Island. It was 3°C at
dawn, and 7°C at noon, when I finished this ink sketch. The sky clouded,
and the wind flung a few flakes of
snow at us. Spring has come slowly this
year. The house yards were greening
and the Willows and Dogwoods
glowed bright yellow and rich red, but
apart from the greens of conifers, the
landscape was still drab, in mute golds,

greys and
browns.

High up there on the brink of the
shore terrace of glacial Lake Iroquois
we could imagine the huge inland sea
lapping at our feet. While the Wisconsin ice sheet still blocked the St. Lawrence Valley, Lake Iroquois filled the
basin of what is now Lake Ontario,
spreading north to the rocks of the
Shield and south to Syracuse, New
York. Lake Algonquin, to the north
and west, filling what is now Lake
Huron and Georgian Bay, spread its
waters eastward and began to drain
into Lake Iroquois through the Trent
Valley. When the ice retreated from the
Hudson Valley, Lake Iroquois drained
south through the Hudson River.
When ice retreated from the St. Lawrence Valley, Atlantic water flowed in
over ice-depressed land, and Lake Ontario below these
bluffs may
well have

Solitary
Vireo
Vireo solitarius
1 Km. e. of Port Hope
bridge, 17 April.

14

dancing bird. After-
wards she drew an im-
pression of it in her
journal.

After visiting 17
stations that night
and hearing Wood
Frogs, Peepers and
Chorus Frogs, we
tried to get some
rest in the Haldimand
Township fishing access
parking lot at the mouth
of Barnumhouse Creek. This
lot was fully used for its in-
tended purpose. There was a constant flow of fisherpeople coming and
going all night in pickup trucks, dabbling bags of coloured Salmon eggs under floats but catching nothing. The air
temperature at dawn of the 19th was
6°C. That night we gave up early when
we heard no calling at Squires Beach. It
was windy with a forecast of cold tem-
peratures and no better wind, so we
drove to Hamilton with a stiff northeast tailwind. We reached Hamilton's
Van Wagner Beach at 23:29, rain beginning, and the thermometer 7°C, before the cold arrived there.

In the sunny morning of 20 April
Fred walked the beach south of our
parking lot, and found little drift except what that appeared to be either
wave-washed Goose droppings or
finely chopped grass clippings. The
beach is coarse gravel and sand in front
of lawn-parks, boulder groynes, recreational buildings and parking lots. He
dredged lavish quantities of fish and
chips from trash baskets, and we

been
brackish. Rebound of
the St. Lawrence Valley established
the eastern end of the lake at the Thou-
sand Islands.

It's difficult to recall our progress over
the next several days from Fred's notes
because we stitched back and forth,
finding our listening sites by day and
running the transects by night. Cold,
windy and exhausting. On 18 April,
before it was dark enough to listen at
the Newtonville picnic area, a Woodcock began its evening display flight
high in the dimming sky. Suddenly it
appeared on the bare ground of a picnic site only a stone's cast from us,
where it performed the other part of its
ritual of territorial defence and courtship. While it was aloft again, we encouraged Jennie to creep quickly toward its dancing place and lie very still
until it returned to bob and strut in
circles, uttering its loud nasal "peent"
call. After two or three such stealthy
rushes each time the bird flew up, her
head was a metre and a half from the

offered them to Ringbill Gulls, who came eagerly, but so did a Mockingbird, always surprising in Ontario, that delicately ate lettuce the Gulls had rejected and picked at french fry pieces. House Finches and House Sparrows completed our bird list. Then we set off for a day of finding auditory stations between Burlington and Toronto. The next day we located the station on Highland Creek, at the Old Kingston Road bridge, and worked our way east towards home, finishing at 22:29, air 4°C, under a clear sky. There wasn't much calling in those conditions.

Fred and Lee Ann got away late on 5 May, but visited 13 stations at the eastern end of the transect, finishing at 02:06, 3 km southwest of Grafton. They heard Toads and Peepers at most stations, and Chorus Frogs, Leopard Frogs, and Wood Frogs less frequently. The next night they visited 17 stations, finishing at 1.5 km south of Newcastle on the west side of the broad Graham Creek valley, and spent the day searching for salamanders and finding snails there and near Newtonville.

They visited 19 stations the next night, ending at Squires Beach. On 8 May, they found two male Toads calling in full sunlight from a drawn-down pond in Etobicoke's East Humber Bay Park. In midafternoon they left for the Mill Grove area along Hwy 2, the QEW and Hwy 6, to establish an auditory station above the Niagara Escarpment. Three kilometres west of Mill Grove the road runs past big excavated ponds fringed with Willows and patches of Cattails, the first big wet-

land area north of the western end of the waterfront. Peat seems to have been removed from these ponds, but there is no sign of bog plants in the vegetation. At dusk a pair of Geese was calling nearby and a Snipe was winnowing in the clear sky. There was a distant chorus of Toads, a scattered chorus of Spring Peepers, and some calling by Leopard Frogs. Then they drove down to Dundas and got lost (as we subsequently usually did) trying to find the Desjardins Canal station.

After 16 stations, the night ended in Toronto near the base of the Leslie Street Spit, at 01:40. One Leopard Frog and distant Toads were calling, and two Woodcock were peenting and flying. One normally hears only at dusk and when the moon is bright. Here there was no moon but the entire area is brightly lit artificially, from the Port of Toronto and around the high stack of the inactive R.L. Hearn Thermal Generating Station. Every time we visited this station through the end of May, Woodcock were peenting, so here they must display all night long through the entire courtship season. In the morning Lee Ann went home by train, and Fred drove to Bishops Mills, stopping at Frenchmans Bay to view the solar eclipse, but too weary to do more.

Fred and I set out on 29 May for an auditory survey during which we had morning meetings with People who had gone to bed before 03:00. This, and the difficulty of sleeping in the cramped quarters of the truck, left us

I can see two small round-shelled Painted Turtles among the angular Map Turtles.

In western Trenton we pulled into W. Bains Park, on the Bay of Quinte, where a Great Blue Heron was hunting among the narrow offshore islands. This park narrows into a long point of mowed grass and graceful Willows, its stoney banks tufted with intensely green tall grass. A couple of gaps in the point are spanned by short wooden bridges. Enormous Carp were breeding in the shallows, roiling vast puffs of mud and thrashing explosively against the tall emergent grasses.

At right angles to this point and parallel to the shore are three narrow stoney islets, remnants of something built long ago. Now they are grown tall with grass, and Redwings guard their territories from last year's *Spirea* and bushy young Willows. Beyond the shade of the bushes some of the stones, many of them on close examination, are not stones at all, but Map Turtles. I noticed the shiny backs of a few Painted Turtles before seeing the piles of Map Turtles they were basking among. The flared shells of the Map Turtles match the fractured rocks. I sat on the lawn to draw them by telescope, and noticed the up-pointing heads of swimming turtles, cruising around the islets, and diving periodically for about 10 seconds. As the sun moved the concentrations of turtles gradually moved to follow it.

able to visit only about a dozen stations each night. Calling was not intense, but the late season species, Green Frogs and Grey Treefrogs, had begun to call.

After visiting 12 stations on the night of 2 June, hearing Peepers at most stations, Grey Treefrogs at only a couple, and Toads and Green Frogs only once each, we awoke at the Wicklow Beach boat-launch. At 08:00 many Cormorants were resting on the groynes and water of the new boat-launch, and then suddenly a great flock, perhaps 400, was swimming in a linear front, diving in relays for silvery fish, likely Alewives. About a hundred Ringbill Gulls were hovering and diving shallowly among the Cormorants.

As I was getting up, Fred walked over to the WRT-sponsored boat-launch pier, which was just mud and rocks at our first visit, but was now a pair of stout, flat-topped groynes protecting a steep concrete ramp. He found a big Milk Snake pounded dead, hidden under a small cairn of rocks. We headed home along the lakeshore and then Hwy 2, with Lilacs in lavish bloom along the roadsides.

3

Royal Botanical Gardens Camp

The mowed lawns of the Royal Botanical Gardens are level green plains cut into the top of the steep dissected slopes of the Escarpment. The slopes are anchored by old tall natives, White Cedar, Red and White Oak, Sugar Maple, Walnut and Butternut, which together form a safe enclosure for narrow valleys that run together like fingers of upwardly cupped hands. Close enough to always hear the wails, drones, booms and clanks of the surrounding cities of Burlington, Hamilton and Dundas, and the roar of Hwys 403, 2 and 6, the RBG is nonetheless high above it all, and large enough to seem a world of its own. Here we enjoy a world of contrasts. The rolling sunny paths of the rainbow gardens are just as tame as the deeply shaded slopes are wild. The steep, leaf-littered slopes of the dark forest are bare of herbage. The floors of valleys and bayshores are lush with Jewelweed, Nettle, Goldenrods, Aster and Loosestrife, ending abruptly at the narrow gravel beaches of the murky Carp-inhabited bays.

To us the garden paths seem under-used, but by day and night there is considerable automobile use, a constant coming and going of vehicles that pause in parking lots momentarily, and others that park for long periods without emitting any passengers.

Royal Botanical Gardens Arboretum, Dundas, 5 & 6 July

On this day of stifling heat and humidity, we begin our summer's work at the western point of our route along the north shore of Lake Ontario. It was really too hot to do much until after supper, when Jennie and Fred bicycled into the Arboretum. She returned with news that they had discovered a few last blooms on the Tulip Trees, and as I followed her to see them, we found a pair of young Raccoons foraging for

sleeping in a cherry tree.

fallen fruit beneath a tree labelled "Amanogowa Cherry," *Prunus serrulata*. They climbed into the tree at our approach, and Fred kept them there while I went back to the trailer to find my watercolours. I couldn't find them. By the time I bicycled back with Jennie's watercolours, one of the 'coon children had fallen asleep on a lattice work of slim branches, and the other was hugging a heavier branch and watching us with bright black eyes.

I had finished my pencil drawing and was reaching for the paints when my subject woke up. I had to walk around the tree with brush, palette and journal page in hand and water in my shirt pocket, following the little animals as they rambled about in the tree, seeking out and munching up the few shrunken sour red fruits that are left at the end of the Cherry season. Sometimes they balanced out on the ends of long thin branches, one following the other, even though the other had left no cherries behind. I marvelled at the monkey-like agility in the way they negotiated tight turns and regained their purchase after many near-falls.

Before I had finished painting they began to be anxious about coming down, chittering tentative Treefrog calls, and murmuring squeaky little question or "may I have permission?" noises. Eventually they both descended to a low crotch in the trunk, just a little less than a metre from my face, and warily crowded each other down the far side of the tree to the ground.

I sit, near the end of 6 July, another day of stifling heat, cross-legged on the ground, painting a blossom presented to me by its low-slung branch a little below eye level. Backlit by evening sunlight, the blooms of *Liriodendron tulipifera*, the Tulip Tree, are ivory cups half full of orange flames. Each goose-egg-size blossom

Tulip Tree

is centred with a pointed, cone-shaped cluster of pistils, pale yellow, fringed by black-edged straps of anthers of the same pale yellow. These fabulous flowers are flagged about by equally fabulous leaves. Smooth and broad and five-pointed, like Maple leaves, but gently filled out in shallow lobes. The heavy twigs curve upward from low sweeping boughs, holding the young seed heads like short tapered candles. Some of the branches sweep the ground, giving the great, full-canopied trees pregnant, gumdrop shapes on the Arboretum lawn. The blooming season, which has been late this year, is nearly at an end, and we are lucky to see the flowers of this magnificent Carolinean Forest tree, just a little north of its natural range.

Borers Falls to Royal Botanical Gardens, Flamborough & Dundas, 7 July

Fred brought Lee Ann, Jennie and me to the Bruce Trail parking lot above the Niagara Escarpment to begin our afternoon's hike along the Bruce Trail from Borers Falls east to the Royal Botanical Garden's Pinetum Trail and down to Rasberry House, the Bruce Trail Association's headquarters in the RBG. A feral Bird Cherry tree gave us a refreshing treat from its lower branches on this humid day of 30°C as we left the parking lot. There we found Black Raspberry bushes too: a wonderful crop this year of uniformly big, sweet berries. Along the road north to the falls, we feasted on sweet, meaty, tender-seeded Juneberries that reminded us of prairie Saskatoons. The ripe berries are bluish purple and the unripe ones glow bright pink and red. Honeysuckles growing just over the lip of the gorge hold up gleaming red berries clustered with op-posite leaves on

purplish twigs, but we know not to eat them.

A cleared viewpoint gave us a glimpse across the gorge of ivory-tan limestone cliffs draped with overhanging Cedars. Right by the guardrail we found a large clump of Big Bluestem grass in tall leaf, a miniature tallgrass prairie. Deptford Pink twinkled tiny magenta stars from short grass underfoot.

The creek upstream of the falls runs like a canal between low natural walls of limestone that step down from grassy banks. We find a few land and aquatic snails in a sparse drift of twigs. Chicory, Bindweed and Hairy Willow Herb bloom from rocky cracks. The fast, warm water rumbles a deep gurgling chant from its rock channel, and we cross the road to appreciate its rushing wild plunge over the falls, holding hands to brace each other as we lean over the brink.

Sketching from the fenced viewpoint east of the falls, I

wish I could show them in motion, the water leaping out into strands that writhe and flatten into clear sheets with lacy edges, fragmenting violently into beads, and further into a dashing spray. A mist veils its thunder into the pool. Behind the narrow plunging curtain of the falls, round leaves of Wild Ginger bathe in the mist on a sloping ledge, rooted in the crumbling clay from a soft grey seam of shale in the brick-like wall of fractured limestone. Dead and dying Butternuts reach skeleton branches up into the curved airspace of the gorge. Young Basswoods take their place and Sumacs feather the far wall. A slender Ash stands there and Lilacs billow from the top, shading the banks above the falls.

We enjoy more Black Raspberries as the trail continues along a field of mixed Oats and Rye. A large *Boletus* mushroom crouches down among Wild Strawberries and tall grass like a hiding fawn. It is a soft-leather-tan colour, and big, almost 30 cm across the cap.

Suddenly through an opening to our right we look down upon treetops in the bottom of the gorge. They look billowy, like an aerial view of a rainforest. Passing under White Oaks, away from the field, we arrive at a viewpoint with a bench and a vista of forest rolling down to a road, hydro line and woods-banked river. Beyond dark treetops bluish with city air, marches a line of high-rise apartment buildings, and then, over Hamilton, smog so thick that it obscures the horizon.

We walk through woods of sun-dappled shade and wren song, past Dogwoods and green-berried Solomon's Seal. Out again along a field, and then down under Birches, discovering Poke Milkweed with long dark leaves and a loose drooping panicle of popcorn-white flowers. Past a large round sinkhole in the rock with poles across it, a big Sugar Maple stands, double-trunked from the roots, and here a window in the foliage looks out across sunny fields and a band of forest to Hamilton Harbour in the haze. The thin causeway-like line of Hamilton Beach is just visible before the lake is lost in the thick air. Leathery soft Bloodroot leaves, round and loop-notched, dapple the ground at the brink of the slope. The tall grey columns of Shagbark Hickory are clothed in short straps of thin bark that lift at top and bottom. Bladdernut hangs three-lobed air-filled fruits like Japanese lanterns, full of yellow-green light, rows of glossy ivory pea-like seeds inside. One of the pair I have drawn has been opened by something, so we can peek at the seeds.

Bladdernut
Staphylea trifolia

21

Out into a splash of sunlight, Sumac and radio noise from houses on our left, and then back into the woods where a green chain helps us down several steep damp natural limestone steps to a lower, more mosquitoey level. Down, down a steep earthen path where, among fallen logs, moss ripples brightly over pitted limestone boulders, like living coral seen from the mouth of an undersea cave. Then the white Bruce Trail blazes are taken over by blue, and we follow the Arboretum Trail east. Now the slope is to our left, carpeted with leaf-litter beneath Maples, Oaks and Basswoods. Soon the forest opens to a sunny glade of young Walnut trees, 20-30-year-old White Pine, and Pear trees with hard green nubbins of baby pears, pink-blushed on their sunny sides. Hawthorns have trunks bristly with long, crisscrossing thorns here, and we passed through a rather spooky thicket of Buckthorn. Up one scaly trunk, mottled with lichens, a Poison Ivy vine presses itself tightly with rusty hairy rootlets on either side like centipede legs.

Down into the valley we go, on a steep path with switchbacks, and the forest is an atmosphere of leaves, many-layered and mottled with sun. The very air is green. At the bottom it is still and moist. A row of Inky Caps line a log that supports the path. Down a gentle slope where the forest floor is as green as its roof, we find several glossy

red mushrooms, perhaps *Hygrocybe coccinea*, nestled into rich green moss on the steep slope beside the trail. Their caps look succulent, like cherry glaze over lemon filling. I collect one to paint, packing it in some of the moss that grows around it. In one of the soft drink bottles that we have picked up after another party of hikers earlier on the trail, I carve a C-shaped slit, pull the "door" open, and after rinsing the container in a creek, settle moss and mushroom securely where they can travel safely and stay moist.

There is exposed, worm-churned soil above the mushrooms, and sprinkled all about we find empty snail shells – *Novisuccinea ovalis*, tweedy-patterned *Anguispira* and low-turbaned white-lipped *Mesodon thyroidus*. We keep finding more and more, as if there has been a rain of shells. They clink together musically in our palms. They *are* a rain of shells, in a way, having been washed down by rain from the eroding bank. We find one live *Anguispira*, solid and cool to the touch, and I'm sure that if we came back at night we could see many live snails.

We walk for a short distance along York Road, which passes under the railway tracks, feeling like frightened rabbits on the short grass beside rushing, fuming cars and trucks. We cross the busy road to the

Hygrocybe coccinea

Royal Botanical Gardens parking lot set about with signs and maps in a meadow of Goldenrod, wild Grape and blooming Milkweed. The area is being reforested by the RBG, signs tell us, and we follow a gravel cart track, glad of the light spitting of rain that moderates the heat of the day, since we've left the cool mature forest behind. The path leads us by a huge old Oak tree. The heavy, open leafy network of its branches is a world in itself, bathing us in a breath of coolness as we pass. We walk over an open hill and under a hydro line. The Evening Primroses have shed their petals and have gathered up their broad pale sepals like the corners of a napkin. A Cottontail rabbit crosses the track ahead. Bobolinks perch among Goldenrod at the brow of a hill, conversing among themselves in little short, twittering calls. Their breasts are so black that at first we thought they were Redwing Blackbirds. They fly away with wings ablurr like bees. Lee Ann picks up a round, glossy, five-banded *Cepaea* snail. Finding these is always like finding prizes, tiny striped Easter eggs.

We pass by a plantation of Pines and up a mowed dirt track from a bridge on the right that we didn't cross. At a branching of the trail we decide to go uphill, and find Deer tracks on the path as we pass between walls of greenery, all kinds of trees above an understorey mostly of dogwood. Ironwoods are decked out with soft blonde pockets braided in hanging tassels. Female Sumacs raise rosy velvet spikes of "hairy berries" but the male

Sumac bushes lift fairy-fine spikes of delicate yellow flowers. We dip into forest shade to cross a plank bridge above the dry bed of a creek with red clay banks and a green shale bottom. The path leads up again and down into another cool shady hollow, where a green band of hard-packed clay on the path changes to red. The path crosses a culvert at another dry ravine and then sweeps us right up into the sunny green-mowed vista of the Arboretum. Through the rolling, sunny grounds of Rasberry House and past an old stone silo, we walk back to camp with a very hot and tired little Jennie. It has been threatening rain at camp, and we see Fred coming to meet us along the Arboretum drive.

As I unpack the vasculum that has travelled in a wet towel and pillowcase tied to my pack, I'm pleased with how

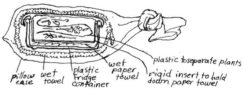

it has kept even delicate flowers moist, cool and intact, layered lightly within the pleats of a strip of plastic inside a snap-lidded fridge container, and humidified by a damp paper towel held down by a frame of bent copper wire. The orange mushroom has also travelled well, in its plastic pop bottle. All I have to do is bend back the door and there it stands, ready for Jennie and me to paint it in our journals.

Grindstone Creek Trail, Royal Botanical Gardens, Burlington, 9 July

I bicycled to the Royal Botanical Garden's Grindstone Creek Trail from the Arboretum this afternoon. Crossing two plank bridges from the Valley Inn Road, I pass several parties of young people fishing contentedly. A father and twin daughters have brought Grandpa out to sit in a lawn chair in the shade of a Cottonwood tree. They are fishing with worms. Bindweed twines about the Cattail leaves to unfurl pink and white morning glory trumpets. Magenta spikes of Loosestrife nod and glow against dark Cattail leaves. Yesterday Fred found the large round shell of an Oriental Mystery Snail floating against the shore, and a juvenile Painted Turtle basking on a log. The bottom is kept well churned by Carp, and the brown water is inscrutable, as opaque as paint. Gulls float demurely like toy sailboats where Weeping Willows trail their long skeins of mist-green foliage into Sunfish Pond.

The first part of Tollhouse Trail is paved, between a low forested ridge and Grindstone Marsh. Wild Grapes climb the Honeysuckles and Cottonwoods toss their rushing tops in the wind. At the Grindstone Creek observation deck in the shade of a large Manitoba Maple, a Redwing Blackbird sings "burgledee" and a fancy-coated Chipmunk flounces from beneath the deck to the tangle of Honeysuckle and grapevine.

Leaving my bike below, I climb wooden steps under long-armed oaks to the hedged and manicured lawn, elegant wooden gazebos and Iris beds of Laking Gardens. I descend to my bike again and coast down Tollhouse Trail past strolling couples, to a flat where the marsh has been filled to the edge of Grindstone Creek, beneath the towering slabs of concrete that support the coming and going lanes of Hwy 2 way up against the sky. Clouds of Foxtail Grass blow silky blonde on the hard-packed clay and gravel fill, and a pair of Mourning Doves leave together, wings atwitter. A young Cottontail watches me from the middle of the path as I scribble notes about its long narrow head and upright ears, set well back, and then it has to leave as I proceed. The path turns to dirt and passes a People-dwarfing stand of the noble grass *Phragmites* with broad blue-green leaves, and very high, the whispers of last year's flower heads. The path becomes woodchip beneath trees, and then boardwalk. A little

Fringed Loosestrife

24

Witch Hazel
Hamamelis
virginiana

dusty-brown sparrow hops rapidly across a few boards ahead of me and then off into the Cattails and Loosestrife where a clear stream trickles. A Waxwing flies round a curve ahead and then comes back to see what I am as I stop again to write. The boardwalk becomes sectional, with wood chips between different levels. Tall Fringed Loosestrife, nodding all over with large yellow blossoms stands in a bed of crisp-edged Coltsfoot leaves, and Cow Parsnip towers above it all with grand deeply-incised leaves and big flat panicles of flowers gone to green seed. The Raspberries on the bank to my left have pink flowers like tiny crumpled tissue roses.

Misled by a side trail, treacherously steep for a bicycle, I'm met by the vivid orange light of a clump of Butterfly Weed and many Witch Hazels, tall and slender in the understorey of the Oak, Hickory and Maple woods. I turn back when this high trail spur disappears. I join the trail again at the bottom and cross a bridge, meeting a splendidly stately Turk's Cap Lily nearly ready to open two of its three pendulous spindle-shaped buds high above my head. A Green Frog calls twice. Water striders keep the sky reflection twinkling. Damselflies with black velvet wings folded demurely above electric blue bodies rest for a moment on the bridge and then flutter away, flirting with each other.

The path climbs a bit to a lookout over a marshy area where Grindstone Creek is still brown and slow, but partly clear and about 4 m wide. The woods here are rich and jungly with an understorey of Grapevine and Sumac, and the slope is steep down to the creek on my right. False Solomon's Seal, Dogbane and Buttercup bloom here, and long delicate pink sprays of Tick Trefoil lean across the narrow path. A Garter Snake slips into the bushy Dogwood, and a Green Frog calls once from a Duckweed-covered pond below the wooded slope on my right. A big Oak tree has been felled across the trail – by mosquitoes as a trap for bicyclists, I think as they catch up with me struggling to hoist my bike over the trunk. Here is another lookout tower from which to view the marsh, partly obscured by Oaks. It is past suppertime, but I paint a watercolour before turning back: Maples with the forest floor sloping up behind.

Cootes Paradise to Carrolls Point, Dundas & Burlington, 12 July
We embarked in our aluminum canoe

Young maple at Grindstone Creek

sketched in black spray paint on the cement pilings. It is very dark under the rail bridges. Then we slip out under overhanging Willows onto the bright reflections of Hamilton Harbour.

Jennie saw a Blackcrown Nightheron fly low over the water. *Nycticorax* – "night raven." To our right, Woodlands Cemetery rises in billows of blackness, and ahead loom the Willows of Carrolls Point, the spit that comes off the cemetery grounds into Hamilton Harbour. The dark water surface is rolling slightly and ruffled by a breeze I can scarcely feel. A Heron complains in a descending call, "Errk-errk-errk-errk." We see something above the water surface as we approach land, and Fred asks from the stern, "is that a snag?" We steer past it, and as the bow crunches onto the narrow sand and pebble beach we shine head lamps on the snag, and it's a young Ringbill Gull, with tweedy back and rough head, looking calmly puzzled, paddling tentatively in the shallows. Geese call tersely, repeatedly, and a pair of Canadas come round the tip of the point to investigate the disturbance we've made. One of them sounds every second, like a watchdog barking at night. Fred disembarks and picks up a clam shell. "Unionids," he says picking up many more old eroded shells of *Elliptio complanata* with pale pearly pink insides. I shove the canoe into a tangle of leafless old grapevine by a tall clump of Purple Loosestrife.

from our Cattail-marsh landing just north of the Royal Botanical Gardens dock and Boathouse this evening just at dusk. These are my notes: Fireflies among cattails. The shore smells rich, rather fishy. The sky is clear. Lights along the highway shine yellow stripes on the dark water like sunlight through fence palings. We are heading for the bridges at the mouth of the Desjardins Canal, with Fred, Jennie and Lee Ann paddling. The bridges are five: three highways and two railways. There are signs warning against swimming and that four lives have been lost in strong current. The beams of our headlamps pick out four sad and sleeping faces

Lee Ann and I press through Grapevines and Honeysuckles to the other side of the point and find there, under

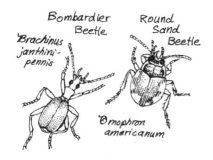

Bombardier Beetle
Brachinus janthini-pennis
Round Sand Beetle
Omophron americanum

a Willow tree and just above the beach sand, a band of green felt – moss and algae together, firm and damp. Stooping to examine it closely by headlamp, I find much busyness of scurrying beetles – glossy slim ground beetles (one pair mates briefly), rapid round beetles with mottled backs, and delicate orange-bodied beetles with iridescent green wing covers, all roving about.

Big glossy grey sow bugs trundle here and there disconcertedly, probably finding our lights much too bright. One has pale yellow spots in a line down its back. A quick red earthworm pokes about at the wet edge of the alga-matted sand. There are two glossy

chestnut-shelled, black-bodied *Zonitoides nitidus* snails crawling on moss and waving their slim tentacles.

Fred has started a beach fire for Jennie to feed with driftwood. Warming my back there, I gaze at the beachline and harbour lights. Part-way back toward the canoe I find the perfect spot to paint from and take out Jennie's wax crayons, squirrelled away in my watercolour set for just this opportunity, night reflection of harbour lights in wax resist. (When I look at it in daylight, it seems pretty garish, but that's what it looked like in the dark, with the help of a dim headlamp to see painting and palette.)

Fred and Lee Ann collect the little clear golden-shelled *Oxyloma* snails active on drifted sticks at the edge of the beach. Silverweed, *Potentilla anserina*, is there in yellow bloom, a ferny-leaved sand-cover with strawberry like runners. The Unionid shells are all old, toe-tinkling shards among the pebbles. One almost uniform consequence of

Hamilton Harbour painted at night

human abuse of lakes and streams is the loss of populations and diversity of this family of large, subtly lovely clams, which depend on fish to disperse their young. The only recent bivalve shells are the Zebra Mussels sparsely scattered through the drift on the very tip of the point.

We leave Carrolls Point at a little before midnight, the fire put out with plastic bags full of water. The water is 22°C and the air is 19°C. Jennie is chilled by the breeze. A train labours rumbling, throbbing, carefully, over the bridge before we thread our way under bridges and pull hard for home.

Caught in our lights, the Nightheron couldn't see where to fly.

Nycticorax nycticorax

North Shore Boulevard, Burlington, 13 July

Just before noon Fred set out by bicycle along the Waterfront route to the east, the first of the afternoon trail segments by which we explored much of the Waterfront through the summer. Where Valley Inn Road goes under the CP tracks, he found a bush of delicious yellow-fruiting Black Raspberries. Unlike the neighbouring black fruit, they appeared to be untouched by birds or by People other than Fred.

He cycled along Woodlands Cemetery's smooth paved roads past the steep path down to Carrolls Point, and out on Spring Garden Road and Hwy 2 to Holy Sepulchre Cemetery, above Willow Point. On the sloping bluff, a forest of exotic trees, Norway and Sycamore maples, and Black Locust, seeded from cemetery plantings screened his view of the harbour. He took Plains Road to the residential parkland of North Shore Boulevard, where he noted a long list of exotic trees: Smoketree, *Ailanthus*, weeping European White Birch, Apple, purple-leaved Norway Maple, Linden, Crabapple, Weeping willow, Norway Spruce, Catalpa and *Ulmus pumila*, the small-leaved Asiatic Elm. One Silver Maple and perhaps some of the a few *Thuja* cedars (though most looked Asiatic) were the only local trees, and there were innumerable exotic shrubs.

He then passed through a neighbourhood of brick houses with Norway and Silver maples, then one of more mixed, flatter houses, and more diverse trees, then down across a bit of lawn to a shallow valley dominated by a curving white apartment tower that looks like a layered white confection or an electrical capacitor. The surrounding lawn bore a notice of application to amend zoning requirements to build another. A gravel-bottomed trickle flowed across the lawn from thickets of Willows, Nettles and Jewelweed.

He came up the hill and down LaSalle Road to Hamilton Harbour and the boat launch ramp, at the western edge of LaSalle Park, where a female Mallard shepherded her brood of half-grown ducklings. On the ramp there were a few Zebra Mussel shells in masses of drifted aquatic plant leaves. Three species of water plants were growing in a metre of clear water over pebbles of coarse gravel: *Anacharis canadensis, Myriophyllum spicatum* and especially *Vallisineria americana.*

The shore of LaSalle Park was thronged with quiet People, Geese and Mallards, with Goldfinches overhead. He saw a few big olive crayfish, many *Etheostoma* Darters that appeared to be tending nests, and Zebra Mussels bound to the undersides of stones by tough elastic byssus threads, but no snails or other molluscs. A track runs up from the shore through woods of White Pine to a lawn where he was pleased to see White Clover and tiny yellow Black Medic in flower, indicating restraint in the use of herbicides.

Out on the road again, Fred rolled downhill through Oak woods to the limits of LaSalle Park, and to Window-on-the-Bay Park, where he found a good view of the Hamilton steel plants. The shore is armoured with massive boulders, above a bottom of algae-clotted rocks, with no evidence of crayfish activity. Cicadas were whining, and a Song Sparrow sang. He continued to the rough lawns of the QEW interchange, and then turned around to head back.

DESJARDINS CANAL and Cootes Paradise, Dundas, 13 July

Jennie and I push away from the canoe landing, east of the Royal botanical Gardens boathouse, and paddle out into the end of the bay to investigate several wire and black fabric enclosures. About 3 metres square, the wire fences appear to be, as Jennie exclaims, "cages for waterlilies!" not to keep the plants in, but to keep Carp out. We saw big splashes even as we approach the enclosures – rooting, roiling, heavy-bodied Carp that have done more damage to these wetlands than an overpopulation of feral Pigs can do to a forest.

On our way to pick up Fred and Lee Ann at the Boathouse dock, we poke into a little cove that is being used as a nursery, its muddy head cordoned by yellow plastic tape between wooden stakes into beds for young emergent plants. The west bank of the cove is lined with paper pots of more wetland plants, waiting to be established as soon as their protection from carp can be secured. When I spoke with Brian Pomferet, biologist with the RBG, he described the replanting and water-level control projects in Cootes Paradise.

Before getting underway we pause to watch Caspian Terns fishing. One gives a croaking call and then hovers momentarily, head with heavy orange bill cocked down till body and head seem folded in half. Then it spirals down like a kite in an eddy, abruptly folds its grey-backed wings and plunges – up again with nothing, orange bill gleaming. A Kingfisher announces his presence with a harsh clatter, and we watch him dive from an overhanging Willow. A Spotted Sandpiper flies low, wings ablurr, occasionally interrupting his "buzzing" to "twinkle."

The constant rush of road traffic comes across to us through the clear evening air as we paddle along a shore forested by Willow, Ash and Black Locust, where Sumacs raise rosy flower spikes from the shadows. We head across the bay, through water the colour of dilute pea soup and coffee, to Hickory Island, abristle with Cormorants. Black silhouettes in gothic attitudes adorn the bare branches that protrude from the top foliage of Oak trees. One Cormorant flies above, impressing us with its large size and hooked beak. We paddle close beneath the island trees and are enveloped in a rich fishy smell. Foliage is spattered with white Cormorant guano, as if someone has been painting the sky without using a dropcloth.

The waterline is felted with green moss and algae, beneath a heavy undergrowth of Sumac, Grape, Honeysuckle, Virginia Creeper, Milkweed, Bindweed, Cocklebur and Purple Loosestrife. Broad bare paths lead up onto the island from the shore. A stiff breeze rises, and Jennie clinging to a Willow branch to moor the boat so that I can write, is alarmed by the chop. So we leave, downwind to the west, along the Desjardins Canal, pausing briefly on Bulls Point to collect a few snail shells drifted in a bed of Silverweed under Willows. We round the point to find a group of RBG biologists watching a Deer browsing Red Raspberries on a brushy slope. They have just completed this season's banding of young Bank Swallows. I sit at the end of the RBG's plastic water-filled dam that stretches away like a huge black leech, to sketch the Bank Swallow colony. We are told there are about 80 parent birds and close to 120 juveniles. With soft cheering and snipped cheeping chirrs they circle and swarm like bees about a hive, weaving an aerial net of defence and celebration of the new-fledged young.

The dam will be used to lower the water level of the wetland behind Rat Island so that the bare mud can be replanted, free from Carp disturbance. The water is shallow everywhere here, our paddles striking mud. The absence of aquatic vegetation, which once filled Cootes Paradise from shore to shore, is glaringly apparent. All power to those who attempt to control Carp and replant the wetlands!

The banks of the Canal project out into the marsh as narrow dikes where

30

dredging spoil was piled when the canal was dug. The opening between the Willows is so narrow that we missed it at first, paddling past nearly a dozen Great Blue Herons standing to fish in the last light of day. They are hard to pick out in the dusk among snags of standing driftwood. A fingernail moon is high in the west against a powder-blue sky, and the smog-haze streaks into greyish mauve above brownish sunset pink. *Nycticorax* the Night-heron croaks repeatedly as he flies with broad rounded wings and no long legs out behind. "Moth-birds," I say, as we see seven in the air at once when we paddle back out through the Blue Heron snags to find the canal mouth.

Now we paddle down the straight, narrow channel, very calm and quiet. A Heron feather floats like a silver-grey boat, riding our ripples and as it drops behind. Fireflies flash in low bank vegetation to our right, and sky light gleams through foliage spaces among dark Willows that line the left bank. The compound leaves of Sumacs on the northwest bank trace tropical silhouettes in the dusk. A Willow leans horizontally in front of us, its young branches vertical, like a

fence. A Green Frog calls from somewhere to the right, and we take a side channel in that direction.

Turning into West Pond, we see bright lights ahead. Carp churn and swirl like ghostly paddle strokes ahead of the canoe. We bump a monster in the night, "Father Carp," and he pummels the side of the canoe in his surprise. Lee Ann yells! A Deer on the bank appears as two yellow-green lamps close together, a long slim orange neck below, and the reflection of its eyeshine in the water as we pass. We stop at York Road, a grassy bank with guard rails, at the yawning mouth of a steel culvert. The canoe is hauled out and the waiting truck backed onto the lawn to receive it.

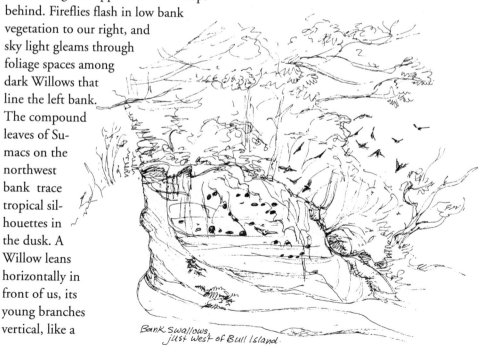

Bank swallows, just west of Bull Island.

31

4

Burloak Park Camp

Burloak Park, Burlington, 15 July
A tower for 60 people nests, across from a long, strung-out shopping centre in the middle of whose parking lot I am sitting to draw. A man, whistling a waltz, walks by with a big English Sheepdog, and small groups of young People pass, engrossed in light banter or deep conversation. On the far side of the parking lot an aggregation of youths careen and flip on skateboards. Cars swish by in a continuous, spaced-out stream, making it difficult to cross the street. A Mulberry tree with dark green, mitten-shaped leaves offers us glossy sweet berries on its lower branches, and long-winged moths swarm to the flowers of a Linden tree. We picked a handful of them, musky sweet, to dry for tea. A 40-unit condominium is planned for the neighbouring lot. A sign advertises it as "shoreline protected." Huge blocks of quarried limestone are built up above the lake like a castle wall in a tale of dragons.

Who protects the Bank Swallows? Is the lake-fill park we see mapped out on a sign in Burloak Park going to take their presence into account?

We walk to the edge of the park lawn. I can hear the soft vibrating cheep of nestlings in the bank just behind me as I sit to paint. Grasses and Goldenrod tangle their roots together into a sod on top of slumping yellow sand riddled with Bank Swallow holes. Below is a layer of crumbling red shale, notched into deep folds by the lake, and below that curve plates of harder shale like cracked ceramic tiles, mostly terra cotta colour, with occasional bands of green. Down into the clear green water I can see the pattern still. The Swallows are gone, and then they come again, casting back and forth and back and forth in the air, showing sooty brown backs, and then pearly white bellies as they swerve and turn, getting closer to their nests each time until my eyes get tired of watching them, and then, if I'm lucky, I see one slip secretly in for 4 or 5 minutes to tend its young. Then, sketching or taking notes, I usually miss seeing it pop out again.

Lakeshore Road, Burlington, 15 July
Lee Ann drove Fred back to North
Shore Boulevard to continue his bicycle
survey where he left off, at the Francis
Road Bikeway, a strip of lawn with
planted conifers that runs north in a
hydro right-of-way, between rows of
house backyards. The brook shown on
maps is a trickle that emerges from a
culvert only to enter another under
North Shore Boulevard. He followed
the hydro line southeast to Hamilton
Harbour at Allview Avenue, finding a
nice view of the Harbour and Skyway.
On an island that supports the hydro
line, many Cormorants crowded in little trees at the bases of the pylons.

He passed under the QEW to the
northwest corner of the open lakeshore
at Spencer Smith Park, a short beach
and boat-launch ramp tucked in
among rocks and seawalls of diverse
ages and origins. On the beach a few
Zebra Mussels were the only shells
among sticks, plastic, and Goose feathers. A short palmate-leaved Hollyhock
bore a single pale bloom on the beach,
the sandy bank was dominated by grey-
green whispy Hoary Alyssum, *Berteroa
incana*, and the seawalls were lined
with low trees of *Ulmus pumila*, a
small-leaved Asiatic Elm.

East of the boat-launch, a narrow
lawn-park parallels downtown Burlington past a straight seawall of steel plates
topped by massive decorative pillars
and chains. At its northeast end this
trail loops out around a little point,
and then turns inland to a short boulder beach.

Back on Hwy 2 he crossed Rambro
Creek, a small embankment-bound
rocky stream of clear water. He turned
rocks and found their undersides scut-
tling with amphipods, which suggests
that crayfish are absent. Perhaps they
are driven out by the greater, dirtier,
flow when storm sewers are active. Big
Zebra Mussel shells were heaped on the
rocky bottom of the stream mouth
where the water sloshes with the waves
on the lake.

He passed a series of balconied high-
rise apartment buildings that graded
down into individualistic houses with
smooth lawns, magnificent Black Locust trees with deeply incised bark, and
many large Maples grotesquely dis-
torted by decades of trimming around
hydro wires. At the southeast end of
Guelph Line Road Fred found a lawn
parkette, with a parking lot, beds of
Snapdragons, and a concrete slab beach
washed by heavy algal slop. A Common Tern danced and finally plunged
into the lake. Like a lighter molecule in
a gas of Ringbill Gulls, its attitude as it
caught the wind after looking down
could have served as a definition of the
word "lilts."

A kilometre farther on he came to
the mouth of Roseland Creek, at Sioux
Lookout Park, thronged by Geese,
Mallards with ducklings, and abundant
Ringbill Gulls, including three dead juveniles and two or three near death.
Gulls and Geese mooch much the same
food from People, but Geese, which are
rarely found dead, eat grass and algae
naturally, while Gulls, whose carcasses
litter the shore, feed on fish and dead
animals which may have concentrated

Bank Swallows and beautiful red and green shale at Burloak Pk.

the lawn from 20 m up in a Silver Maple. It is interesting to count black and grey Squirrels, as the black is only a colour variation of the Grey Squirrel species. He was to be back in camp by 20:30, so he hurried past Shoreacres Creek, where three Goldfinches bathed and a female Mallard attended four young. He stopped again to glance at Appleby Creek, overshaded by feral Norway Maples, and then continued to camp.

Shoreacres Creek, Burlington, 16 July
Lee Ann, Jennie and I began our afternoon's explorations at the mouth of Shoreacres Creek, sitting on a stone wall, watching a mother Mallard supervising the activities of her 10 brown and yellow ducklings, and feeding Apple cores to the local Canada Geese. We are glad that this land remained wild as the McNichol Estate and has now been acquired by the city. An interesting Willow stands in its moss- and algae-covered root wad, completely surrounded by water, more than two metres from bank and wall. The whole base is sculpted smooth and round by rocks in the waves, and by winter ice. On shore, Ash trees tangle their bare roots like hands grasping each other among the shifting cobble stones.

pesticides and other toxins to a dangerous level. At the creek mouth he found our first fresh unionid shells, two *Anadonta grandis* amid a scattering of Zebra Mussels. He turned many rocks in the knee-deep shockingly clear water of Roseland Creek, but saw no sign of crayfish or living fish or molluscs. This site may be scoured by flows from the 'water purification plant' just upstream.

He continued past more houses and more pure grass lawns, though the median of Lakeland Crescent, evidently not treated with the herbicides used on private land, did support some Clover and Plantain. He was surprised there by a black Squirrel that thumped down to

The creek's mouth, cobbled and lightly furred with algae, soon becomes too deep to wade, so we walk its bank on a Raspberry-lined path through a meadow and back to the creek. We climb down into it over the bodies of Hickory roots. The undersides of the stones we turn in search of crayfish are alive with large Planarian flatworms, and aquatic isopods like quick little sowbugs. There are also tough leathery egg cases like flat black bubbles glued to the stones, and crayfish too, little *Cambarus bartoni,* some soft-bodied from recent shedding.

I explain to Lee Ann that crayfish reproduce by internal fertilization, which can only occur while the female's shell is soft after shedding. Then the opening of her seminal receptacle can receive the male's pen-like first pair of swimmerettes. The female's swimmerettes are uniform small flaps. When she is "in berry" they are clustered with large brown eggs, and after hatching the baby crayfish hold on to her swimmerettes for three moults before they go their own way.

Here the forest is a sun-dappled green tunnel for the creek. We duck beneath two of the horizontal trunks of a huge old Black Willow that has split in several directions. Its branches rise up from the recumbent trunks and it spreads its canopy like a one-tree forest. A Cardinal twitters and two Redwing Blackbirds engage in a singing duel. On the banks Spotted Jewelweed is coming into bloom and round-leaved Burdock towers above my head as I stand on creek gravel at the foot of the bank. The new burr at the top of an elegant tall green Teasel is soft as a baby Porcupine. The ribs of its leaves have sharp needles underneath, and the spines on its ridged stalk are curved like cat's claws. Lee Ann finds three more crayfish as I stand and admire the way a not-yet-opened Jewelweed flower hangs closed like a red-spotted Goldfish, its tail curved under its tummy.

We wade on, and now can see the Lakeshore Road bridge through Grape vines on a Honeysuckle that arches above the creek. A "fossil" bicycle is partly buried in the broken shale of the creek bed, and now the anoxic sulphury smell of storm sewers wafts down the creek from pipes emptying beneath the bridge. We decide to cross the bridge rather than wade under it, walking over dried-out strips of sod laid around planted Aspen saplings. Upstream the water is clear and fresh over a creek-bottom of broken red shale. We soon come to a deeper, mud-bottomed channel and a partial dam by a large shady lawn with People's voices, a difficult stretch to navigate without trespassing.

Upstream of this we find more crayfish, and Lee Ann learns how to hold them without getting pinched. A small Sucker scoots into a hole in the rocky bottom. The bankside Willows plunge their dark roots into a solid matrix of rootlets and reddish earth, firmly upholstered with moss like a carpeted bench along the creek. Under the water, Willow roots come out like straight snakes, nearly a metre from the bank, long

Mallard ducklings

Anas platyrhynchos

ropes that fray into orange-tipped root-lets. The creek trickles over a knee-high horseshoe falls of algae-stained shale, from a broad shallow rock-bottomed pool ahead of us, fed through a bed of jumbled flat rocks below a wooden footbridge with concrete footings. A Cardinal calls "Perpidee perpidee perpidee poopidee poopidee."

We walk the leaf-carpeted bank be-low a steep slope of Oaks and Maples with the back of a garage and a chain-link fence at the top. We are entirely surrounded by residential neighbour-hoods, but it is surprising how little of them we see, how wild the creek can seem through so much of its length. A huge old Hickory tree spreads over the bank with bulging, swelling roots that remind us of flowing lava. Sheathed with purple and red flaky bark a big Pine stands almost a metre through at chest height, among big Maples and Beeches. Each tree seems like a monu-ment, and we are glad to be here.

A delightful creek like this can easily be thought of as "dirty" by People who know it only at the bridges, where wa-ter trickles or gushes from the storm sewers, carrying the sulphurous gases given off by microbes that work in the absence of light and air. The creek soon exhales this smell; aerobic bacteria take over, staining the mud and pebbles rusty, and streaming algae filter the overload of nutrients. Only a little way downstream snails and planarians graze, fish nibble, and crayfish browse and scavenge, and the diversity of stream life has come a long way toward its natural level.

We cross an arching wooden foot-bridge to the east side, and see the west bank upstream lined with sand-filled oil drums set in concrete to keep the bank from changing position. Enchant-ers Nightshade raises pretty spires of tiny white flowers, and Red Baneberry its stalk of vermillion fruit. The trail goes beneath dark draping Norway Spruces and then returns to the creek bank under an open canopy of Walnut and Maple. A crowd of heavy-trunked Grape vines are surrounding and kill-ing a Black Walnut tree and I look up the Walnut trunk into a maple-like fo-liage of Grape leaves.

The path shortcuts a bend in the creek at a sunny twinkle of yellow-flowered Fringed Loosestrife, and we sense that we are approaching another bridge. A thicket of slender-trunked Hawthorns spreads a romantic rooflike canopy of small dark leaves set in a flat latticework of branches and twigs. I find a Cepaea snail sleeping in the top of a Goldenrod plant and pick it to draw, as this is the first time I have thought about how well their habit of pulling leaves about them hides them from above, from a bird's view.

The musical sound of falling water from the storm sewer echoes beneath our last bridge, so we return south to Lakeshore Road and back to camp.

Bronte Creek to Shell Park, Oakville, 17 July
Yesterday evening Fred, Lee Ann, and young Jason Hand took the canoe down Bronte Creek from Petrocan Park to the Shell Pier and most of the way

along the lakeshore to camp. They looked for crayfish in the clear stoney-bottomed riffles banked by tall Willow and Walnut woods, finding *Orconectes propinquus* and a few young *Cambarus bartoni*. *O. propinquus* is our boldest crayfish, often active in daylight, boldly patterned with a dark abdominal band, while *C. bartoni* is a uniform brownish colour, often burrows in gravel far below surface stones and is active in the open only at night.

Our canoe party had only gone a few metres before the channel deepened and lost its clarity, widening into quiet water between raised shores with Cattails behind. They gathered Basswood blossoms for tea from an overhanging tree where the east bank turned to Oak forest.

Approaching the marsh below our "12 Mile Lookout" auditory station, they paddled through a patch of Yellow Waterlilies, a quarter of them still in bloom, and noticed little plastic pellets dotted all over the leaves, presumably washed there in the last storm sewer spate. Passing Cattail beds on both sides, they came to where the west bank rose steeply, with a triangular outcrop of neatly bedded red shale, and saw a small Woodchuck walking carefully down the talus slope beside the cliff.

A current swept them into a Cattail lagoon on the west side, toward a pair of Mute Swans with two grey cygnets. The cob immediately bristled into full-feathered display with folded wings

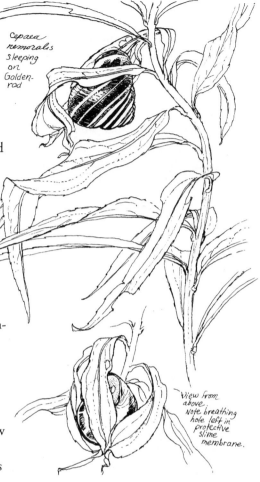

Cepaea nemoralis sleeping on Goldenrod

View from above. Note breathing hole left in protective slime membrane.

cocked forward and quivering, beak down and head feathers all raised into a brushcut. He swam in threatening circles close about the canoe. As the intruders retreated, he zigzagged behind, and when they finally turned out into the main flow of the creek (the strong flow into the lagoon had eased), he thrashed across the creek with blanket-heavy wing strokes towards a flock of Geese, driving them up onto the shore. When Fred tells this story, he calls the cob "Butch."

They paddled under the Hwy 2 bridge, glimpsing a colony of about 15 Cliff Swallow nests, then into a forest of sailboat masts, where docks extend down to the next bend in the river. The west bank is a Willow-graced lawn-park. Farther down the river mouth, motorboats were moored, and in and out among them baby Mallards swam after their mothers. As the canoe paddled out of Bronte Harbour, past a man playing polkas on an accordion, and People walking, and People fishing, they saw a dark cloud bank and felt a long swell on the open water. Glass-green water rolled and twisted the canoe a little as each swell passed, but the air was still calm, so they decided to continue on, past armour-fronted house lots. Then the swell increased, and the whole sky clouded over. As the canoe approached the long Shell Pier, Jason noticed the first narrow fields of ripples on the water, so they decided to land the canoe there, not fancying the uncertain passage under the arches of the pier and along the steep seawalls beyond it. The waves breaking on the steep gravel beach were not yet half a metre high, but that seemed plenty for the canoe. Lee Ann pulled the bow in with only a little water coming over the stern, just as the mercury-vapour lights on the pier were beginning to glow.

The little beach just east of the pier is formed of terraces of cobbles and flat shingle, with big garden-

elegant clumps of Japanese Knotweed. Seventy-nine "goose people" walked down in single file from the lawn of Shell Park and spilled onto the water like a ribbon of viscous fluid, out onto the lake and, still in single file, under the first span of the pier, west toward camp, just as the canoe would have done if the sky had been calmer.

Burloak Park, Burlington, 18 July
It rained this morning, so the Canada Geese didn't come here to graze until this afternoon — resting, watching, preening, pulling at the grass with their beaks, doing all of those goosy things with pastoral contentment and serene confidence. I love to see big creatures grazing in open places, and feast my eyes on the light and shadow defining their shapes. They have no need for camouflage in the open as they trust in general flock watchfulness. Nothing People do threatens them, but they explode thunderously away from unleashed Dogs.

Appleby Creek to 14 Mile Creek, 18 July
Fred resumed his eastward survey this morning at Appleby Creek, upstream of Hwy 2. The shallow clear brook runs through a patch-park of trampled deciduous forest on clayey soil. He found one adult female *Cambarus bartoni* under a rock in the deepest pool of the creek. A few

Cambarus bartoni

dozen heavy-bodied chub-like 10-15-cm fish crowded under stones or rushed for alternative cover when disturbed, and there were also smaller brassy-coloured minnows. At Hwy 2 he found anoxia and amphipods under stones below the three storm sewer outlets, and a faint sewage smell. The stones were embedded in sand and gravel and blackly anoxic underneath, and there was mossy algae growing on them, which wasn't necessarily a water quality difference from the site upstream, as these rocks were exposed to the sun.

In the afternoon he continued east from Burloak Park into Oakville past Shell Park and through residential neighbourhoods. Sheldon Creek flows across Hwy 2 in a lawn-park, clear above the bridge, but cloudy below with a moderate inflow from storm sewers. He crossed Bronte Creek and turned lakeward on Bronte Street to the Waterfront Trail, a gravel path between apartment buildings and the newly-enlarged harbour.

The harbour is a wide basin enclosed by a limestone boulder breakwater that is not on our topo maps. Flakes of blue-green and bacterial growth floated in patches like the leaves of emergent pondweeds, which Fred at

first took it for. A Common Tern plunged into the water, Pigeons zigzagged down to the water's edge, and People and Dogs wandered past. The narrow beach on the outer side of the breakwater is felted with a brown blanket of coarse alga. Blooming Purple Loosestrife was the dominant species among diverse herbs and young trees on the shore at the base of the breakwater. The mixture of species struggling for space among the limestone boulders included Silver, Manitoba, and Norway Maples, White and Cottonwood Poplars, at least three kinds of narrow-leaved Willows, Coltsfoot, Carrot, Jewelweed, Bindweeds, mints and Burdock.

A path of fine gravel and white dust, dampened where adjacent gardens were being sprinkled, continued between a diversity of apartment buildings and the sloping seawall. This is a real waterfront trail, a path only for walking and bicycling, not in a park, running between the water and otherwise-used lands.

Turning sharply north, the trail followed streets for a while, then at Coronation Park Fred found the first extensive beach we have seen, composed entirely of skipping stones. The bagful of drift he gathered from above a felty blanket of dead green algae excluded Pine and Norway Spruce cones, baseball caps, rags and swimming trunks, but included a gilt lace circlet, duct tape, lids of paper coffee cups, seams of plastic cushions, a woolly woven fleece garment lining, shoe leather, cigarette filters, a link from a waste-tire doormat, a bandaid, a scrap of orange carpet, various bits of plastic, a Mallard speculum feather, bark from a narrow Birch branch, a Peanut hull, a scaly *Juniperus* twig, and many twigs and coin-thin pebbles. The only remains of aquatic animals were three Zebra Mussel shells and skull fragments of an Alewife.

He came to a boat-launch at the north end of the park and watched People tending tiny one-person motorboats.

Across the road Fred walked into a mature Beech forest on sandy soil. These magnificent untrampled remnant woods, with abundant leaf litter, are part of the grounds of a sewage treatment plant. He waited out a shower of rain under the shade of a spreading Red Oak tree there, and then visited one of our auditory stations on the bank above 14 Mile Creek, south of the mouth, a steep-banked valley in deciduous woods, filled with the green plumes of Ostrich Fern. Under the threat of increasing rain he retreated to Hwy 2 at Wolfdale to wait for me. I reached him just as he was getting drenched, with lightning blasting only 2 km away. We got his gear off the bike, and the bike on the rack on the truck, and drove back to Burloak Camp, where it had not rained at all.

OAKVILLE

Coronation Park to Oakville Creek, 21 July

Fred and I are setting out to bicycle east through Oakville from Coronation Park. Over an enclosure of fine gravel sprawls a large wood and plastic play structure which children rove over and through like happy monkeys while their mothers hover in groups at the corners. Juvenile Ringbill Gulls wander around, wishing there were more to eat, fixing us with large dark eyes and whispering plaintive peeps. An adult patrols, yellow-eyed and thick-necked among them, to chase them away from any scraps of consequence.

I turn toward the beach, and beside a short jetty of huge rocks, find bathing-suited children throwing stones into the lake over a ribbon of felty green algae. On thin mangrove-like roots more than a metre high, a Willow tree stands grotesquely on tiptoe, framing views of the lake above its rootbound, wave-worn root ball, and reaching its neat young summer leaves out over the lapping wavelets. Geese preen busily over their broken reflections. There must be at least 250 Geese in this park. A big flotilla of them just off the beach attracts more down from the lawn. "Mom, look at the million Geese!" a boy shouts, pointing. His mother is watching where she steps, trying to keep her shoes clean. In the shade of a bush of Sweet Sumac where I write my notes, a large Monarch investigates a clump of Pussy Willow.

As I explored Coronation Park, Fred crossed the street to the woods of the Halton Sewage Treatment Plant, and lifting cover carefully beneath old Beech, Sugar Maple and Red Oak, found two red-backed and one lead-backed *Plethodon* salamanders. He noted many sowbugs under logs, few snails, and an understorey of Witch Hazel and White Trillium. People have brought gardening waste into the untrampled woods, and a few trees have been cut.

Starting east along Lakeshore Road, we come to a bridge, and look down on 14 Mile Creek, splashing and chattering with storm-sewer enthusiasm, wide up to its Willow and Purple Loosestrife banks, and the colour of skim-milky tea. Fred says it was clear before this morning's downpour. Life in a creek such as this is threatened by each heavy rain, as water from storm sewers carries sediments and waste into the streams from roofs, streets, and parking lots. Many animals may be crushed or swept away by the spate, and sediment clogs gills and covers or fills living space. The flow is very low between storms because the water has already rushed at once into the lake instead of filtering into the ground to feed plants and springs.

We bicycle past interesting houses of various sizes in a tall-tree suburban woodland, at times through the fumes of herbicides that kill broad-leaved plants in lawns, admiring the wonderfully braided ridged bark of full, fine-foliaged Black Locust trees. We pass Appleby College, its mowed grounds rolling down to the lake, and then a row of big Sugar Maples, much older than the houses behind them. On a sunny lawn beyond a stone wall, a pair of Crows pants with beaks agape and their head feathers all raised.

Where the shady suburbs give way to the sunny main street of the commercial district, we turn lakeward down small streets with quaint little houses to a park surrounding a water treatment plant. Most small parks along the urban Waterfront away from creek mouths are founded on municipal ownership of land around some element of the plumbing system: water intake or filtration, or pumping or treatment of sewage. A path heads east along the shore from here, above a limestone seawall and below a rock-shored bluff overlooked by a line of houses. We pass little groves of fairy-tale Paper Birches, and come to the deep-shaded foot of a flight of wooden stairs, up which we carry our bikes.

At the top of the stairs we cross a bit of lawn to follow a broad brick path as it curves toward a tall flagpole rigged like a boat's mast. This bold landmark is set on the crest of a high knoll, looking down upon the crowded forest of masts in the mouth of Oakville Creek, and the long pier that juts out into the lake. A cyclist with a telescope watches a cluster of small sailboats about a kilometre off shore. One of them capsizes and the others circle about as if offering advice. We hear faint shouting, and eventually the sail comes up.

A steep gravel path takes us down into Shipyard Park. Captain James

Andrew's shipyard, ca 1880-1900, certainly didn't look then as it does now: red, white, blue and green canvas sail covers below a thicket of aluminum masts. A paved drive leads beneath the Hwy 2 bridge to a restaurant patio with bright umbrellas and painted iron fences. On a short, parched pelt of lawn grass a single Deptford Pink blooms among a few round leaves of Geum, missed by herbicide at the foot of an Ash tree.

Discovering the steep access road up to the bridge, we pedal hard to the top, and cross the bridge to the east bank. Two blocks back toward the lake, we find the grounds of the Erchless Estate, and four Heritage buildings which now make up the Oakville Museum. I decide to paint the corner of the Customs House which faces the lake, viewed across a small park with a play structure and picnic tables, as Fred walks down to the east side pier. I ask the lady who sits here, attending a playing child, if she will stay for a while to be painted, so after making a general sketch, I finish her first.

Children and parents come and go, and the only one who shows interest in my work is a woman with an European accent. She compliments the painting and draws her reluctant granddaughter closer to see.

Fred returns with an account of his own observations. The creek, pea-soup murky and napped with goose feathers, is dotted with Duckweed. On the other side of the pier the clear water of the lake is a deep blue-green, and sun-ripples lace brilliantly over large green-pelted rocks. On the harbour side of the pier, the white limestone boulders that front the town's rescue facility are bedded well above the water line with fine

Stachys tenuifolia
Hedge
Nettle.

spring drift in which scattered herbs have grown up, including sprawling plants of the mint *Stachys palustris*, Woundwort, with many full spikes of pink bloom.

To the east the boulders are clear of drift and dazzling in the sun and below them is a narrow beach of exquisite skipping stones. Fred spent some time engaged with them as I painted the Custom House. He was attended by young Ringbill Gulls which seemed not to have known splashes that weren't fish. They wheeled and landed on the water repeatedly, one coming close to being hit by the next throw.

We biked back to camp through Oakville's summery downtown, past planters brimming with flowers and crosswalks defined by rows of bricks. Eastward, Hwy 2 is a tree-lined street with large houses, interesting fences, lawns that often support some broad-leaved herbs, and magnificent trees – including a European Beech, *Fagus sylvatica*, with smooth muscular trunk spreading a parabola of leaves high against the sky, a dark russet tint drawn over the green, a tree I would revisit Oakville to see. As we were examining a Cicada we found dead on the road, Lee Ann and Jennie came by in the car to pick us up.

The Esplanade, Oakville, 24 July
The Esplanade is a segment of public shoreline between the ends of two small streets east of the centre of town. A narrow white gravel path runs down the centre of the strip of lawn. Some of the yards are screened from view by fences, but others are not, sharing the free, open feeling of community lake edge.

A variety of seawalls here protect the shore from erosion by the lake, and I decide to draw tumbled rough boulders at either end of an elegant sloping wall of poured concrete edged by a railing. It is a calm evening with just a little breeze. The lake is cross-marked with low swells from wakes of offshore boats and smoothly rippled like a waterworn stone. Rosy-white gulls blink into shade as they fly toward the dark shore, among them a Caspian Tern. The white sails of little boats also gleam in the sun. On the lake's edge, beyond birds and boats, the hazy blue shapes of Toronto's distant towers indicate its presence to the west.

At the edge of the bluff, plants have escaped from garden waste. The rich green foliage of *Polygonum cuspidatum*, Japanese Knotweed, dominates, with clumps of Rhubarb, Jerusalem Artichoke, Comfrey, Apple seedlings and a domestic Iris.

A flock of thirty Canada Geese cruise placidly by, and then some linger to see if we have anything for them. When I look up from my drawing, one is standing on the flat stone just before me, tilting its head a little to the side and regarding me with a shiny dark brown eye. Others dabbling nearby tip their white bottoms and emerge with long dark

Dogday Cicada

Tibiacen lyricen

streamers of coarse-fibred algae. They don't seem to have grazed the top of the bank here, perhaps because the bouldered bluff is too rough for them to climb.

A Blue Jay calls from trees above the bank and a House Wren is scolding. Three Great Blue Herons appear from offshore. Majestic and rosy-grey in the evening light, they stroke slowly westward. The Geese move on, following the rest of the flock as they poke along the shore to the east. The gulls and terns have ceased fishing and retire offshore, settling for the night like a dusting of white specks on the surface. A Redwing flies west along the brink of the bluff and so does a fluttering Monarch, followed at intervals by two others. The rosy colour leaves the sky and lake suddenly as the sun dips behind a cloud bank, and five Nightherons wing rapidly over the darkening lake.

Some very late Cicadas begin to rattle in the dusk like evening-calling frogs. Their high nasal buzzing swells and then fades away. The city across the water begins to sparkle with lights, seeming nearer than the ghostly grey shapes I had drawn earlier along the horizon. As I rustle with my packing up, Fred says he has heard a Nighthawk "beep" in flight, the first we have heard from a species that has sadly declined since we lived in Toronto in the 1970s, when they were always overhead all evening long.

Burloak Park, Burlington, 19 July
Today we leave for our next camp in Port Credit. As we lift the coolers, the damp pavement underneath scurries with the glossy brown bodies of European Earwigs, which we call "Masters of the Universe." Insinuating their flexible, pincer-tailed bodies into everything, no matter how high above the ground it is stored, they seem to be as strongly attracted to snug places as they are to things edible. Broadleaf Plantain, another European introduction, which often takes over from lawn grass in heavily used areas, has proven the ideal campsite groundcover; its ground-hugging oval leaves show no signs of nearly a week of trampling. The Geese that clip the lawns are like a family to leave behind.

5

Port Credit Camp

We are camped by Port Street behind marinas and shipbuilding yards, behind a house from which a family friend runs his business. Manitoba Maples shade our trailer, and we walk one block north to Hwy 2, the busy main street of Port Credit, to buy ice for our coolers and fresh rye bread from a delicatessen. A Skunk ambled across our camp yard late one night. Concerned for our coolers, I imitated the voice of a large Dog to hurry the little black and white vagrant on its way, though it was certainly a resident of much longer standing than I.

Oakville to Mississauga, 22 July

Picking up our trail in Oakville, Fred found *Cambarus bartoni* crayfish in rocky Morrison Creek, which runs through a Willow-wooded valley corridor. Water was pouring in from drains under the Hwy 2 bridge span, and the creek was cloudy with silt. The only vegetation was sparse stringy algae, and there were lots of Mayfly nymphs under stones.

Oakville Art Gallery Park, Gairloch Gardens, at the creek, is about as big as a one-houselot park gets. There are tilled beds of flowering herbs and shrubs, and in one a carpet of the edible wild herb *Portulaca oloracea*, Purslane, sprawls beneath a colourful dis-play of cultivated blooms. A pair of captive Trumpeter Swans cruise by the creek mouth and the seawall-hardened shore. Doubtless they have some role in the plan to replace escaped exotic Mute Swans with this North American species, which may have bred around Lake Ontario before the days of the fur (and feather) trade.

At the next bridge, Fred found Joshua Creek to be a silty-rocky creek in a Willow-wooded corridor. *Cambarus* crayfish were common, including one female with a few eggs, and he found one dead juvenile of a second species, *Orconectes propinquus*. A trail system runs north from the highway, but Fred took paths and roads downstream along a narrow strip of lawn-park between the valley and new housing subdivisions. On the brushy brink of the wooded valley a couple of clumps of Pink Jewelweed were blooming, and Black Raspberries were conspicuously unharvested, spoiling on the canes, while birds were at least present, as he heard Robins and Blue Jays.

He came out to the lakeshore and looked down the steep clayey path to the mouth of Joshua Creek, which looked fascinatingly forested, perhaps a wilder creek mouth than we have yet seen, and won't see again until Highland Creek.

As he crossed into Mississauga, the character of land use suddenly changed. A field of Tomatoes by a garden centre was the first agriculture we have seen along the waterfront, then there were a lumber yard, motel, arrays of radio antennas, wild scrubby woods, and up ahead a big cement plant. Avonhead Creek ran in a concrete channel, a mountain torrent coming down steps northwest of the road, and along a sluice-like channel to the southeast.

Past the cement plant Hwy 2 turns away from the lake at the industrial filigree of an oil refinery. A thunderstorm ended his excursion there and I found him waiting in a bus shelter.

Jack Darling Park, Mississauga, 21 July

From a bench by the lake Lee Ann and Jennie had a view of the reconstruction of Jack Darling Park into perfectly rounded sloping lawns. Medium-size shrub trees were being brought down from leaning stacks on a flatbed, loaded onto a backhoe to be dispersed across the grounds. The only previous features kept in the new plan are the romantic Weeping Willows that drape the path along the shore.

Most of the beaches were overlain by deposits of specially sized gravel, but on the one sand beach left they found a drift of plastic, twigs, and Gull and Goose feathers. Animal remains included Alewife fragments, vertebrae of other fish, the skull of a passerine bird, a few crayfish carapaces and chelipeds, and five Zebra Mussel valves. The only

snail was a Great Lakes Horn Snail, *Goniobasis livescens*. After the rich drift we sampled east of Toronto this spring the absence of land snails along the urban shore is astonishing and appalling.

Turtle Creek is a fairly shallow, fast-flowing creek with a rock bottom that winds its way through a swampy area thick with Cattails, Arrowhead and Purple Loosestrife between Jack Darling Park and Rattray Marsh. They found a few juvenile *Stagnicola elodes* snails in it but no crayfish.

Rattray Marsh, Mississauga, 21 & 23 July

The Rattray Marsh reserve, hemmed in by crowded houses, is a mosaic of remnant habitats. Lee Ann and Jennie entered the open Cattail marsh dotted with newly flowering Purple Loosestrife, along the new Waterfront boardwalk. Redwing Blackbirds were click-ticking and flying as wind stirred the Cattails, Poplar leaves clattered, Cicadas whirred and delicate wine-red Dragonflies flitted past.

The mouth of the marsh was closed by a 1.5-m-wide bar of large rounded stones. In the outermost edge of the marsh, there were many minnows and four large Carp trying to nose a way into the lake.

A dozen old Hemlocks shade a winding creek in its rocky bed. The steep banks show slight, vertical erosion, like a miniature sample of the hemlocked west coast of Vancouver Island. Lee Ann and Jennie found no crayfish or aquatic snails there, only one *Cepaea* shell fallen into the water.

Along one of the little streams there is a small grove of thriving Witch Hazel, with many clustered fruit nuts. Sugar Maples, Red and White Oak, and the occasional White Birch shade the slope and path, but the edge of these remnant woods is never far away, and huge mats of Grapes, already with tiny pale green nubbins of fruit, crowd into the trees. They followed a smooth dirt trail up a steep forested slope, finding no salamanders or snails under the few logs, and arrived in waist-high Jewel-weed at the top of the slope.

West of the marsh the land opens into a dry meadow of sedges, Golden-rod and Elderberries, buzzing with insects. The gleaming orange berries of a Honeysuckle bush caught Lee Ann's eye at the Old Poplar Row entrance to the reserve. She and Jennie were discovered by mosquitoes in a shady upland plantation of mature Pines and slender White Birch.

Two days later, while Fred cycles east from Port Credit to Etobicoke, Lee Ann, Jennie and I come to Rattray Marsh for an evening of landscape painting. From a wide place on the wooden walkway we look across Cat-tails waving and open water glinting in the evening sunshine, to the high wooded northwest bank, where houses peek between the trees to overlook the marsh.

Out in the middle of the marsh something shines very whitely against the shadowed far shore, a tall figure with a long thin neck. A large white bird, standing like a Great Blue Heron, with the sun bright on its back. Lee Ann assures me that its plumage is pure white. She has seen it catch fish with quick darting strokes
of its long
neck,

47

and it must be a Great Egret. Although a southern bird, it can sometimes be seen on its brief northward migration to the southern Great Lakes each year after breeding.

Past the end of the boardwalk, a footpath leads us beneath a line of lake-edge trees tangled in Grape vines and out to a charming little beach, where we skip smooth flat stones out onto the wrinkled surface of the lake. As Lee Ann hunts for snails and Jennie visits with People walking Dogs on the boardwalk, I look toward the lake across the level green field of the Cat-tail marsh and begin to paint.

Port Credit to Etobicoke Creek, Mississauga, 23 July

Fred set out at 17:30 along the shore to Marie Curtis Park. Just east of camp he passed the partially demolished starch plant. Only a few days ago I had hoped to draw the stark rearing shapes of the broken buildings and elevators, but they are melting away like a time-lapse movie of archeological decay, and by the time we left this camp there was only a field of bricky rubble.

He cycled past the plant to Tall Oaks Park, which occupies one houselot at a sewage pumping station, its beach bounded by protruding concrete walls. Continuing northeast, Fred found Hiawatha Park to be another public green space based on a water-processing site. Small boys standing on the fractured concrete seawall averred that the lake was salt water, with sharks, and were not corrected by an attending adult. Outside the seawall a

Spotted Sandpiper burst out from jumbled boulders, 29 Geese loafed on cloudy-clear green water offshore, and two Caspian Terns were over the lake.

Half a kilometre through a residential area, the trail abruptly plunged into a forest-like Sugar Maple woodlot, part of the Adamson Estate, an old residence and lands made into a park. A grassy promenade extends along the shore past a large residence-like building to a shingle beach layered with algal felt. In from the shore, Fred sought snails and salamanders in a trampled woodlot but found only a few slugs, *Deroceras reticulata*, and two old *Anguispira* shells. This woodlot has a very mixed canopy of native trees: Red, Sugar and Silver Maples, Yellow Birch, Ashes, Oaks, Black Cherry, Basswood, White Pine and Hemlock. The herbs Garlic Mustard, Jewelweed and *Geum* are each dominant in different patches of the forest floor. There were signs warning of Poison Ivy, but he saw only scattered Jack-in-the-Pulpit plants, which also have three leaflets.

The asphalt bike path goes east over our first non-vehicular bridge, a span of rusty steel over Cooksville Creek, its mud-in-milk water covered by Geese, to the Lakefront Promenade Park, a recently completed lake-fill. The western headland of this park is a "naturalized" old field, laced by paved bike trails. Patches of Canada Thistle were blooming in dense patches among Goldenrod stands. Ashes, Austrian Pine, Spruce, several species of maple, Aspen and Locusts are not the trees we see as natural colonists along the shore and are too evenly spaced to look natural. What will it look like in five or 40 years?

The ground looks moderately fertile, the sod is dense, Song Sparrows are singing and Mourning Doves calling, but something is wrong. Leslie Street Spit with almost no species variety looks wilder than here. Perhaps there are no Voles to influence the plant community, or perhaps the appearance of wildness depends on the extravagance of natural reproduction and competition.

A red snowmobile-like motor craft crashed and splashed around in the choppy waves offshore as Fred continued around the headland and down the sorted pea-gravel beach of the inner bay to the central peninsula of the park, devoted to parking lots, boat launches, picnic pavilions and forests of sailboat masts. Exotic shrubs are planted in monocultural patches in tilled beds. Gulls gathered instantly when food was thrown, and garbage cans loaded with Chicken bones, buns and cheese provided plenty of material to save from becoming landfill.

The headland of the eastern peninsula of the park is encompassed by a Stonehenge-like harbour wall that runs out from the silent four-stack hydro plant next door. Fred found a brick-paved area thronged with children and parents, busy about picnic tables, water sprays, and a tall play structure made of planks. People fish from the boardwalk facing the Lakeview Thermal Generating Station. A heavy-bodied juvenile Great Blackback Gull, the first we have seen, loafed among Ringbills.

The Waterfront Trail was under construction to the east, so Fred detoured along a street crowded by flat-topped industrial buildings. He came out to a veritable Ayers Rock of piled coal, that feeds the Lakeview hydro plant, scored by gullies and glowing yellow in the setting sun, behind young Cottonwood trees with dark green leaves rippling paler undersides in the stiff breeze. A Mockingbird sang and a Killdeer called.

The trail across Serson Creek and into Marie Curtis Park was still barred, so he continued along the highway to the road entrance to the Park, and thence over rolling lawns down to the peaceful lakeshore lawn-park.

CREDIT, 26 July The day started bright and sunny. After sketching out the positions of buildings and boats in pencil, I decided that the rest of this scene consists of details too fine to be sure of, so Fred cycled back to camp for the telescope, and now I'm checking every line that I draw, through the scope: its angle, its length, and where it begins and ends. Shortly after I'd set up the scope we had to anchor the umbrella more securely as a brisk wind from the northwest lifted its pole out of the cleft between rocks where I sit. Little waves began to dance in the harbour and the sun disappeared behind threatening black cloud. We packed up and biked the two blocks back to the trailer just before Port Credit was

sluiced by a summer downpour of "white rain," the kind you can't see through.

After lunch we went out in brilliant sunshine, only to find more clouds coming and the breeze so brisk that we had to find a branch and a cement block to hold the guy-rope. I continued to draw until Fred brought the truck and then I rested there for a while, as Fred searched out a perfect little board for me to stick my paper on, solid enough to keep it from lifting and rattling in the wind.

This has been a nearly impossible scene, under nearly impossible conditions. Fred recorded my carping about the shapes of the boats: "These Salmon boats are exceedingly hard to draw! They're all angles. No grace to their construction except perhaps in the hull. They seem to be cobbled together out of features, fittings and gadgets, none of which look like they were made for each other and no line follows another."

A man comes to show us a "16-pound Brown Trout" that he has caught from shore. He opens a black plastic bag, and a fish of tremendous proportions fills the bottom of the bag, a modest head in one corner and a big speckled body swelling out from it. "Full of minnows," he says.

After my drawing is finished we walk out to the mouth of the Credit River, finding the stone and concrete fortifications of the shore so different from a natural river mouth which constantly shifts its banks and bars.

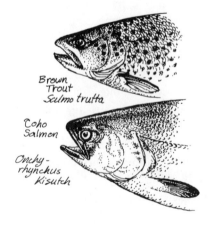

Brown
Trout
Salmo trutta

Coho
Salmon

Onchy-
rhynchus
kisutch

50

6

King's Mill Park Camp

We are camped in the lot of the boat launch of King's Mill Park, one of our auditory stations. Toads were the only anurans that called here this spring. During the week we camped here we heard no calling, and saw no frogs.

Etobicoke, 28 July

At noon Lee Ann took Fred and his bike back to Marie Curtis Park. A graceful soft-plumaged clump of Willow trees stood beside the beach under a soft grey stratocumulus overcast, while a 25-cm surf gently broke at their feet. The mouth of Etobicoke Creek is guarded by steel-sided piers with black railings and paved with asphalt. A juvenile Ringbill Gull caught a fork-tailed 15-cm fish on the lake and gagged it down before other Gulls came to harass it.

On the sand beach just west of the creek mouth Fred found a profuse drift of twigs, plastic, and cigarette filters, raked up onto the lawn in big piles. A couple of Horn Snails were the only aquatic animals and a couple of striped *Cepaea nemoralis* the only land snails. Flotillas of Geese loaf upstream on the creek and motionless fishermen trail their lines from the Goose-grazed banks. He headed east past rows of little brick houses, narrow lake-shore parks, and apartment buildings to the hook-shaped fill-built western peninsula of Colonel Samuel Smith Park, which has grown, since our topo maps were drawn, from the publicly owned lakeshore of a water treatment plant and a psychiatric hospital.

He crossed causeways and fields of weedy herbs on gravel fill, planted with Austrian Pine and Silver Maple and beds of shrubs, and the cracked clay ground was only covered by a sparse tracery of minute herbs, grasses and clovers, doubtless grazed down by Geese. A fire hydrant stands guard over a flat where 200 Ringbill Gulls were loafing, and, heads all together like compasses, an orange-billed Caspian regiment

A lake-washed selection of nature and artifact

51

was airborne before the Gulls went up in an irregular cloud.

Across the water were docks and the masts of sailboats. The water was green and the visible bottom was broken rock felted with green algae. From the blue metal bridge over the oily storm sewer inlet to the harbour, a brick trail led past many exotic trees and bushes and continued to the base of the eastern peninsula of the park as a hard clay trail.

The peninsula still showed its "bones" of concrete, asphalt and decomposing shale. It was pleasant to see that birds and plants were pushing ecological succession along. Starlings and mixed flocks of House Sparrows and House Finches rose up from the ground. Some of the blooming Carrots were purple-flowered, and Scentless Chamomile, *Tripleurospermum inodorum*, was the dominant herb. He found one plant of Musk Thistle. The beaches, almost bare of drift, seemed to be mostly made of gravel aggregate crumbled from rounded asphalt slabs, which led him to wonder how the complex hydrocarbons of asphalt affect the lake.

Heading out of the park to the northeast, he passed a narrow ditch with a sparse stand of aquatic plants, and a muddy lagoon of Banff-green water, which communicates with the lake through a culvert. Clumps of both *Typha latifolia* and *Typha angustifolia* had been planted in the lagoon and were badly trampled by either People or Geese in their abundance.

Then the waterfront route twists northeastward among small apartment buildings, varied houses, and patches of lawn-and-bench parks above boulder-armoured banks. A man had hauled three flour sacks of bread and rolls into Prince of Wales Park to distribute, as if it were his duty, to stolidly pecking Geese, keening Gulls and a few Pigeons.

At a two-bench parkette at the end of Lake Crescent the view of the Toronto skyline was softened by the trees of Toronto Island. The water near shore was a slurry of green algal strands, and an orange Cat was killing a young Rat among the boulders. Northward, the Mimico shore is shadowed by apartment bluffs, where children played on shelflike balconies, and the waters edge of parkette beaches was green-black slime, the sand beaches crusty with Goose feces, and the lawns littered with feathers. The lakeshore here seems exhausted and out of balance, far from the refreshing influence of meadows and marshes. Waterfront regeneration is a big task, but we hope it has already begun.

Before returning to camp, Fred rolled out onto the fill-built peninsula of Humber East Park, where he noted three flour bags in the garbage baskets at a traditional Goose-feeding site, as if the man he saw at Prince of Wales Park runs a regular bread route.

Colonel Samuel Smith Park, Etobicoke, 2 August

While Fred is away at home, Jennie, Lee Ann and I drive to Colonel Samuel Smith Park for a late afternoon visit. Terns fly with their sharp black-capped

heads angled down as if their orange bills are heavy, always keeping an eye on the water below. They call "Yeeeow! Yeeeow!" Four cruise past, over the clear green shallows, over the neck of land, above the bare masts at the yacht club, and on.

This place is wonderfully spacious – lake under sky – the roar of the city behind me. Silent sailboats tack slowly below roving gulls on a serene blue ribbon that stretches nearly all around the horizon. Colonel Sam Park is a new lake-fill peninsula scalloped by many bays, still very rough and barren in places, with patches of soft blond Wild Barley grass brushed by the lake breeze, a scruffy "seaside meadow" with Goldenrod, Wild Carrot and the daisies of Scentless Chamomile. Larger boulders from the fill are used to shore the sides of points between bays

Chordeiles minor — a memory sketch

and to border a network of curving gravel roads.

In the distance to my left, the lights of Hamilton twinkle at the edge of the lavender lake beneath the pewter-grey sky. Before me, marking a rocky headland, stands a concrete tower painted yellow, and then the lake stretches on until the towers of Toronto mark the skyline, Scattered white flecks offshore, are Gulls settling to sleep. Several late sailboats reflect pink sunset on the bright triangles of their sails. Strobelights on the side of the CN Tower flash like synchronous fireflies and all of the other city lights brighten as the daylight fades. Buildings on the near shore behind me are partly hidden by dark masses of trees, and green gaps of lawn come down to seawall and boulder-shore.

As we turn to go, I see a dark shape land on the path. Sneaking up on it, I make out the shape of a Nighthawk, long wings extending past the tail, round head with no distinct beak. We are about 2 m from it when it flutters, and then skims up in V-winged flight. It comes down again behind us, raising its wings, wrists together, to land, and the white wing-bands clearly visible. Then it sits quietly again as Jennie approaches within 2 m.

Something hops among the spaced-out plants of Queen Anne's Lace as we continue toward the car. I hop too, and catch a small greenish-tan Toad. I mark its body length against my journal folder, 35 mm. It is either this year's toadlet, very well fed, or more likely a yearling, and small for its age. We haven't seen any plausible breeding habitat here, just a few water-filled ruts and the trampled pond Fred described at the northeast corner of the park.

King's Mill Park, Humber River, Etobicoke, 3 August

Tall, dark, pointed-leaved plants of *Impatiens glandulifera*, the Pink Jewel-weed introduced to North America from Asia, lean toward light from beneath the maple canopy of the slope. Their long stems are five-sided and have strong red joints like Japanese Knotweed. The young growing leaves have long shiny red teeth standing straight up from their edges. Each plant, almost shoulder-high, is topped by a fountain of large pink flowers nodding from long slim petioles.

Each blossom is a tube for small Bumblebees, who clatter their wings against the upper part of the corolla before creeping inside. Their wings, flatly folded against their backs, rub against a caterpillar-like protuberance that bears white pollen along its middle. Behind the corolla's showy front part hangs a cup or capsule-like part into which the bee has crawled. A small green hole at the very end receives the bee's tongue, supplying nectar from the yellow,

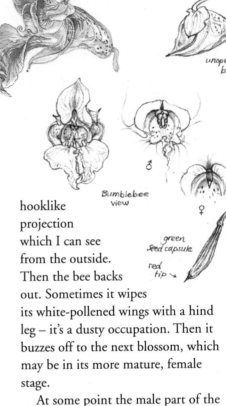

unopened bud

Bumblebee view

♂

♀

green seed capsule

red tip

hooklike projection which I can see from the outside. Then the bee backs out. Sometimes it wipes its white-pollened wings with a hind leg – it's a dusty occupation. Then it buzzes off to the next blossom, which may be in its more mature, female stage.

At some point the male part of the flower must fall off, or be bumped off by a bee, for we pulled one off, and there, inside it, was the female part, a down-curved green stylus-like stigma. Its white tip receives pollen from the bee's wings as they rub past. I can see this happening in a neighbouring blossom as I paint my male flower.

The unopen blossoms hang like flat, shiny purses. The open flowers show their gorges like dragons' throats, with red and yellow fire inside. I find this awesome and compelling as I gaze into it from a bee's perspective. After the stigma receives pollen and the grand pink corolla wilts and falls away, the green seed capsules lengthen and swell. Their sides lined smartly with five white stripes, and tips turned red as if dipped in blood, they grow until they are ready to explode at a touch. Seeds shoot in all directions, in one violent convulsion, and all that is left is a curly tangle, corkscrewed strips of pod.

I first saw these wonderful, huge Jewelweeds, at the parking area in the northern part of this park, where Bloor Street and the subway tracks cross above the Humber River. Beside the bridge we found a surprisingly tall patch of... Parsnip! Tall, green plants with broad deeply-lobed leaves, and on some of the new growth, slept a glossy bright Japanese Beetle. It tried to fend off our attentions lazily with one shiny black-lacquered hind leg, but I picked if up anyway, and so I have painted here, another introduction from the Orient. The Jewelweed is spreading, but the beetle is no longer the pest it once was.

King's Mill Park is a lawn-park along the Humber River. Behind me, a bike path carries a steady stream of cyclists and rollerbladers, gliding swiftly along the smooth pavement. The entrance from the Riverwood Parkway is very steep. I watch a girl glide solemnly down, standing very still in her rollerblade boots and enjoying the rushing the wind of her progress. Her way back up, though vigorous at first, is punctuated by long rests on the curb.

Grazing Canada Geese call to each other about coming over here, and

1cm.

2x life size

Japanese Beetle

Popillia japonica

where you should go next. They fly close overhead, wing feathers rustling like stuff satin capes. Dogs are not allowed to chase the Geese, but sometimes little children do. Ringbill Gulls walk straight-legged about the boat-launch and parking lot, the older ones chasing the younger with necks low and mouths agape, waiting for People to bring bags of bread to feed the Mallard Ducks that mill about the boat launch. Herons haunt the Willow shade of the far bank, waiting for fish to rise to the surface of the secret-grey-green water, and Kingfishers watch the water too, from overhanging branches of Black Willow and Manitoba Maple.

Cars pull into the parking lot, bringing Dogs and children to run on the grass. A family carries bags and coolers across the lawn to one of the few picnic tables. In the centre of the vast green lawn a father plays kick-the-ball with a toddler. When a motor rumbles to life, we presently see the boat glide by, muttering quietly, downstream from the yacht club, and then all the other boats rock gently at their little plank docks. These are all motor craft, for the bridges at the mouth of the Humber River are too low for masted boats.

There is not much shade in this park, though it is bordered by steep woods. Below the houses that overlook the park from the brow of the river valley, a steep earthy bank is scattered with dead leaves that drift against Avens and Japanese Knotweed in the

55

cool shade of Oaks, Hickories, Maples, and feathery-leaved Locust trees. In places *Anguispira* and *Cepaea* snail shells join the litter of sticks and leaves. My feet crush mint at the edge, as I duck beneath low branches and out onto mowed grass again. A culvert leads beneath the roadway, and its storm drain trickle seeps through a small round bed of tall Cattails. Then there's a narrow band of shade beneath Willows and Silver Maples that line its path

Heading down river, where the overhanging Grape vines and low boughs of Manitoba Maples make secret shady vestibules for ducks, we pass a secluded sandy bank where a mother Mallard sits guard before her fledglings who are cuddled together for a late morning nap. We slip up close to a dusty-dry Painted Turtle basking on an old arching Willow log. The red stripes on her wrists show as she turns abruptly and drops into the water. Leafy tips of young Grape vines creep down among the stones shoring the outer bank

down a gravelly bed, before it slips out into the river by a lush sunny bed of the native orange-flowered Jewelweed, *Impatiens capensis*.

Humber River at King's Mill Park, to Toronto Harbour, 29 July

Packed for a trip down the Humber River and across Toronto Harbour, we put the canoe into grey-green water at the boat landing just down from the yacht club, and paddle across to visit a young Great Blue Heron perched on a barkless branch. We come within a couple of metres before it becomes anxious, and, raising its wings from its slim brown and white body and straightening the "S" of its neck, it departs, to stand with the Geese on the lawn by the boat launch.

of the river. Sumacs and Manitoba Maples shade the shore, with Oaks high above. We see a swimming mammal, which proves to be a young Groundhog, nose, eyes and ears above the water, jerking with the effort of each paw stroke. It pulls itself out at a dark cleft among the stones and disappears, not even pausing to shake. One thinks of *The Wind in the Willows*, and how the Mole became accustomed to river life.

We pass high purple banks of Loosestrife, and glide into a lagoon where a turtle is basking on a floating stick. We scan the shore to count four Painted Turtles. A Heron, disturbed as we entered the lagoon, resumes its stalking, step by careful step, before a bank of sunny Loosestrife. It uses the full length of its neck to get a good view in front, then strikes and misses. Nearby a Tern dives and lifts with a small fish which it swallows in flight.

Heading back into the river, we smell a toasty-sweet breeze from the big Christie bakery. The east bank is low, a bed of *Phragmites* grass tangled up with Loosestrife and Grape, and then Cattails too, while on the west, after Willow-hung banks cascading with Grape vines, we pass a shore armoured by rocks caged in wire gabions, and residences at the river-edge, with terraced gardens, elaborate decks, and docks raised by ropes and chains.

The eastern bank opens into the Humber Marshes, and Fred notices the bright yellow colour of a bed of Dodder, clotting Bindweed and Cattails together like lively golden spaghetti. Stepping ashore to spy for turtles, Fred exclaims, "It's just a blanket in here!" Leafless, this delicate golden-stemmed vine parasitizes other plants. I pick a scrap of it, fastened to the stem of a dead Bindweed blossom, to draw in my journal. Continuing across the mouth of the lagoon, we can hear the faint rush and roar of the city. Passing islands of Cattails, we come to a high sandy bank, with a Kingfisher hole beneath its grassy lip, then two iron-grated storm sewer outlets in a shaly bank. A dark-leaved bush of Buffaloberry, Soapberry or Soopolallie, *Shepherdia canadensis*, reminds us of the Boreal Forest, prairies and western mountains.

The west shore is a wall of tall hybrid Cattails. We pass a pair of kayakers as we enter a lagoon there. A Great Blue Heron crosses to join a companion beneath Willows that edge the parkland between the lagoon and the Humber sewage treatment plant that we can smell on the breeze as we paddle north into the lagoon. A Night-heron hovers against the wind and lights at the curtain-like edge of Cattails, where a basking Painted Turtle is so thoroughly pelted with green algae that we have to approach it closely to be sure it is a turtle.

Continuing down river we pass a big Black Willow on the left bank just before the bridges, where boys are preparing three kayaks to launch. The bridges are four, low and straight, with green-painted girders. In their welcome shade Barn Swallows cheep and swoop overhead, and I count 20 nests sculpted of mud against the insides of the girders, while Fred gathers up spring drift that has been protected from the summer's weather here. We slip out from under the bridges in brilliant sunshine, into the mouth of the Humber, past tall buildings that remind us of laser printer cartridges set on end, and between the pair of many-angled white abutments that will soon support the arched footbridge of the Waterfront Trail. Here is Lake Ontario, beyond a long line of concrete breakwaters lined with white gulls. We pull up on the sandy beach of the first of a series of beach parks along the curved shore.

The others disembark to look for drift while I catch up on my notes and watch a Monarch Butterfly resting on the sand. When it holds its wings together they show sand-coloured undersides, nearly invisible on the beach. Faced into the wind, it draws a single line, like a stick among the beach drift. Then it spreads its wings half open for a few minutes, catching the sun's heat on black veins and back, and the next time I look it is gone, on the next leg of its journey to Mexico. Butterflies cool down as they fly, and must bask between flights to warm up. A little down the beach a Tern flutters, dipping and splashing in the shallows. Even though they dive for their food, they still bathe like Robins!

Far along the curve of beach, the Sunnyside pavilion shines white under its red roof, and farther still rise the apartment towers and office buildings of Toronto, and gleaming silver like a flying saucer on a skewer, the CN Tower. The traffic on the Lakeshore is muffled almost to silence, downwind from us, but a dull, distant roar reaches us from the centre of the city itself.

Hoisting my big blue and white painting umbrella for a sail and sunshade, we paddle inside the line of breakwaters. Three Great Blackbacks are twice the size of the Ringbill Gulls they stand among. A young Blackback with brown-patterned back plumage pecks at something underfoot. We paddle in to see what it has: a 20-cm sucker, frayed and

half-eaten. The gull waits in a little bay nearby, washing its black Raven-like beak. Deft and tiny, a little Sandpiper struts under the breast of an unconcerned Ringbill Gull, probing the wet sand rapidly with its long black bill.

Under way again, Jennie runs along the beach. The water is clearing so that we can see the sandy bottom and patches of narrow-leaved Pondweed. It looks swimmable, as we pass the big swimming pool where many people splash chlorinated water about, but only one small boy wades in the lake.

The canoe rocks a bit each time we pass a gap in the breakwater. We land against a jumble of paving stones in a patch of shade below a parking lot, so that I can lie down and rest my unsettled equilibrium while the others turn stones and chunks of concrete to look for crayfish.

They find three large female *Orconectes virilis*, the larger two with black lesions where appendages are missing, and the carapace and chelae of a larger individual with similar black lesions. They find a blueish male *O. propinquus* too, smaller than the *virilis*, and with characteristic dark-backed abdomen and slight ridge along the centre of its nose-like rostrum.

The bare "porches" before the lairs of the crayfish are conspicuous in the bright green algal fluff of the bottom.

Embarking again, we see ostrich-

Dodder
Cuscuta
grovii
choking
Bind-
weed

like plumes of the pondweed *Potomogeton crispus* rising into clear water from the bottom. Passing the rowing club we find pondweed that doesn't look as lovely, a rowboat heaped high with a tangled mound, not appreciated by rowers. Austrian Pines are planted along the bike path, and now we begin to see preparations for tomorrow's Caribana festival: bright canvas pavilions, whirring generators, portable toilets, towers of canned beverages, and vans labelled with the brand names of beers.

Farther ahead, the tall domed cylinders of Ontario Place loom like, as Fred says, "a farm of silos." Lakeshore Boulevard rushes close along shore and the "calls" of an ambulance are answered by Canada Geese. Then we hear the screams of riders coming down a water-log slide as we enter the fantasy world of Ontario Place under a white lacework of arched foot bridges, among little red paddle boats, driven by the bobbing knees of their occupants. The big central sphere looks like a giant ping-pong ball with a net wrapped round it. Its only rival in grandeur is the broad fa-

Orconectes virilis

cade of Exhibition Stadium facing the lake from our left, flanked by huge light standards. The sun knits lively patterns of light on the white hull of *Cloud Nine* as we paddle by with our notebooks, crayfish net and field guides, past pleasure yachts and even a floating bank. Then, emerging beneath a bridge, we face the towering grey warship *Haida*, decked out in flags. We pull the canoe out to portage across the causeway that provisions the fantasy entertainments of the island.

A little farther on, behind breakwaters, where the walls are bearded with green algae like a deep shag carpet, a young Nightheron stands, looking like a small, hunched-up Brown Pelican among Ringbill and Great Blackback Gulls and three Terns, one of which utters a buzzing, begging call from a floating tire.

Then we brace ourselves and canoe into the chaotic wake-and-chop of the Western Gap, past the Island Airport and beneath the shadowy walls of disused Canada Malting grain elevators.

Orconectes propinquus

Wakes from passing boats reflect from the seawalls so they come at us from both sides and Fred has to steer this way and that to meet them. Jennie is frightened at first, but, growing used to the motion, gets up and whoops for more. The canoe dips and bucks alarmingly at times, but we ship no water.

A red tour boat motors past, dressed up like an old steamer, with tall arched windows outlined in gold and a tall black false smokestack, and after it, a yacht so stubby that it seems to be just the nose of a boat. Ahead we can see our destination, the green upper storeys and glassed vestibule of Queens Quay Terminal. Entering the harbour we pass right beneath the bow, it seems, of a tall three-masted ship, motoring along with sails hung out. Finally we round the stern of a big boat and turn into the quay beside our building, where we hope to moor in quieter water.

I hold the canoe in the slip at Queens Quay Terminal while the others go up to get the mail, watching the fascinating, ever-shifting ladder-and-doughnut reflection of a dockside apartment tower and drawing it in my mind. The gunwale of the canoe keeps catching under the side boards of the dock, so I have to reach down from where I sit, 2.5 metres above it, and fend the gunwale off with the flat of my paddle until the others come back. I'm relieved to be off again, as we had moored in a water taxi's stand. It's even trickier finding a parking place downtown by boat than it is by car. From the water we can look right up Bay Street into the heart of the city.

Now we paddle briskly past the ferry docks and strike out into the open harbour. Sailboats flit back and forth past the long, treed shore of the Toronto Islands. We paddle through a flotilla of bobbing Papayas and green and red Bell Peppers. The Redpath Sugar plant whirrs away, a cluster of buildings, ductwork and elevators beyond its docks and trucking lots. Past a long empty dock lined with big tractor tires, we turn at two big rusty blue-black freighters. Beyond them is the opening of a narrow channel, the mouth of the Don River, which we will not have time to explore.

As we followed the Harbour's east side, my easily disrupted equilibrium finally caught up with me and I had to paddle with my eyes shut. I peeked occasionally at a long straight dock and a wide landscape of empty, weed-grown lots and brushy fields with occasional factories and elevators. The diesel fumes of passing barges and tugs lay on the water, contributing to my queasiness. Finally we went through the Eastern Gap and turned east to Cherry Beach to see little silver fish flashing through clear water in and out of billowing algal forests on a bottom of sand, stones, and bricks.

After we beached the canoe, Jennie and I went by taxi and subway to bring the truck from our Humber River camp. Fred and Lee Ann walked the artificial sand and gravel recreation beach, admiring the green skyline of the Leslie Street Spit and the sunset beyond harbour buildings and the CN Tower. They found only three Monarch Butterflies, a dragonfly, a Zebra Mussel shell and one worn fragment of a Unionid mussel shell dead in the drift, but sticky-footed *Trirhabda* chrysomelid beetles climbed up their clothes, apparently washed up on the beach from the Goldenrod fields across the Outer Harbour. The wakes of marina-bound boats went rolling across the sunset reflection in dashed lines until they broke on the beach in a long series of low waves.

Ward's Island, Toronto Harbour, 3 August

As Fred drove back to Toronto from home in Bishops Mills, he listened at auditory transect stations along the way. Spring calling from wetlands is winding down and the frogs are beginning their fall calling from meadows and woods. Along the Waterfront he heard nothing at one station and Green Frogs at five, Wood Frogs at one, and Peepers at two. He arrived in camp at dawn, exhausted, as we were preparing to leave for Toronto Island by ferry.

Jennie, Lee Ann and I climb to the upper deck to enjoy the fresh lake breeze. We sit on wrought iron and wood-slat benches and pull on the jackets we'd brought in expectation that the harbour would be several degrees cooler than the city. The ferry landing on Wards Island looks familiar and friendly in summer, complete with a relaxed smattering of people meeting and leaving, and the bike rack, half full of mostly old and serviceable bikes. I am reminded of visits I made to my friend Elisabeth, years ago.

HE "streets" on Ward's are the same as I remember, narrow paved paths, crowded by trees, bushes, and the yards of well-loved little houses that nestle among jubilant beds of Begonias, Pansies and Marigolds. Umbrellas that match the flowers shade little round yard tables, and from quaint porches, box planters and hanging baskets overflow with bloom. Between these houses are plainer ones, built as cottages long ago and not changed much except by the addition of plumbing.

I explained to Lee Ann and Jennie as we looked for Jess's painting class, that pretty well all of the houses are inhabited year-round, even though Harbour winters are severe and everyone has to be bussed to the ferry at the island airport when the Harbour ices in. Housing on the island is in demand, especially by artists and writers, and there are fewer houses now than there were before expropriations by the city in the 1950s and 1960s. Centre Island now is park, and part of Algonquin Island too, but I would rather see gardens of flowers and vegetables around modest and eccentric houses, and paths through long grass and wild grape to the beach than wide expanses of lawn.

Toronto Islands used to be a barrier peninsula of dunes and wetlands that protected the harbour, fed by the sediment swept west from the eroding Scarborough Bluffs, but the flow of sediment was disrupted during the 19th century, so the main part of the peninsula became an island, and with

Sunset from Cherry Beach

the construction of Bluffers Park and the Leslie Street Spit the flow of sediment was cut off entirely, and now the beaches are starved for sand and eroding away.

We feel so far from the harshness and rush of the city, and everything here is people-scale. Jennie splashes in the lake in the midst of a group of children and sunbathers as I sit, painting, behind a girl who is also painting. There is a commotion among the children as someone spots a large Garter Snake. They are interested but not afraid, and by the time I put down my paints to come and see, it has escaped unharmed. Jennie says it was black and yellow, not one of the pale coloured Garter Snakes which are peculiar

to the Toronto Islands, a colour Fred describes as "lamb gravy," nor the white-chinned black, melanic form which also occurs here, said to have been introduced from Long Point. The Islands also enjoy a healthy Toad population which makes the evening air thrill with their calling each spring.

This is an important stopover place for migrating birds. Muggs Island, another of the Toronto Islands, is a nature reserve, where Fred and I have helped to band Sawwhet Owls.

7

Leslie Street Camp

Lakeshore and Leslie streets, Toronto, 4 August

Last night we moved east to our auditory station on the Outer Harbour Headland and listened without hearing any frogs. We were trying to find a level place to park by the road, when the Harbour Police stopped, thinking we were stuck in the ditch. They advised us that it might not be safe to camp there, due to the frequency of "vagrants" on summer nights.

This morning we awake in the Port of Toronto, a declining industrial area, but with enough industry to make the heavy grey air an assault upon the senses. We have a land breeze, not freshened by the lake, and there are few trees to filter it with their leaves. Rain threatens, and beyond a chainlink fence at the end of the parking lot, a solemn line of vehicles escorts an unmarked tank car on a flatbed truck in an ominously careful procession that I watch with bated breath, hoping it arrives safely wherever it is going, and that its contents remain contained once it's there.

A Monarch butterfly beating west against the gusty breeze is thwarted by the rusty chainlink fence. It makes several attempts to surmount it, and then is lifted over by a greater effort and a new wind. Over the fence it lands in a mowed field of regrown Chicory flowers. Another Monarch comes by, and surmounts the fence more easily, and then they both come back and hang together on the pale globes of bloom of a Milkweed that has pushed up beneath the fence where the last mowing didn't reach. Two Cabbage Butterflies twinkle by, and a few moments later all the butterflies are gone. Fred watches a mowing crew shred the flower stalks off Narrow-leaved Plantain along curb and fence. With the Plantain grow Chicory, Birdsfoot Trefoil, Butter-and-eggs, Horseweed, Goatsbeard, Canada Thistle, Dandelion, a *Potentilla*, Carrot and a clover. Rain begins to fall and the mowing crew breaks for coffee and doughnuts. A burst of wind tosses the crowns of a row of Cottonwood, Ailanthus, and purple-leaved Norway Maple at the east end of the lot and then just as suddenly subsides.

This was apparently the lull before the storm. Fred had retired to the trailer. Exit mowing crew, leaving their tractor parked under shelter of the Gardiner Expressway ramp. Enter a tremendous green-sky thunderstorm out of the north, and a man from the Toronto Economic Development Corporation came to lead our entourage to a one-night camp in a harbourside lot on Cherry Street.

Cherry and Commissioners streets, Port of Toronto, 4 August

Rust-black twisted snakes of cable as thick as my forearm sprawl beneath a great white derrick used for lifting boats out to dry dock. Lighter cables wound on four big drums are fenced in beside a little brick building. These cables have reached up to the horizontal arm of the derrick, way up at the top of the tower, and pulled it back, and four monstrous cables come down, their ends looped through sturdy U-bolts on the gunwales of a tug boat. The cables are taut, steadying the boat that they have hauled up to sit propped on an assortment of beams and posts. A man is on his back beneath the dark red painted hull, grinding at metal with a whining electric hand tool. Nearby a long low building is lined with truck trailers. Huge bales of crushed cardboard, mostly compacted beer cases, lie in an untidy row where they were disgorged from a loading bay at this end of the building, and a truck backs up a concrete ramp to receive a few of them. A low ceiling of cloud obscures the tops of Harbourfront buildings as if they are cloud-wreathed

mountains, trapping us between rain-laden cloud and wet asphalt.

We spent a rainy, windy night in our little trailer, as if it were a docked boat, at our first camp in the Port of Toronto. This morning promises a better day, and we watch gulls walk among puddles as we pull up the trailer struts in preparation for a move to our proper camp. Raising our minnow traps from the green water at the dockside, one from the bottom and one from mid-water, we find no animals in the wire traps, but they bring up scraps of pale algae and an alarming chemical pungence.

Leslie and Unwin streets, Port of Toronto, 5 August

We have a large space to ourselves in a gravel parking lot at the base of the Leslie Street Spit. Our neighbours across Leslie Street are a sewage treatment plant, a public works office and fenced-in allotment gardens. At the broad end of our triangular lot is a boat repair shop, and through the long fence along the back, Jennie watches trains loaded with scrap metal rumble and

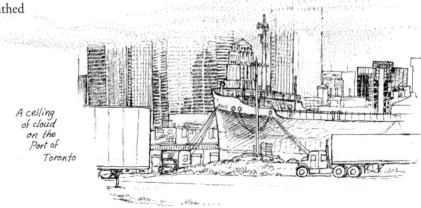

A ceiling of cloud on the Port of Toronto

64

creak along the tracks at the foot of a grassy berm and a high brown metal wall.

This wall shields a recycling operation of some kind from our view, but not from our ears. The tops of cranes sweep the sky and we are at intervals enveloped in the sounds of breaking glass, clashing metal, the groaning and grinding of heavy machinery, and huge metallic booms. There is no lack of sounds from other directions: lawnmowers, the banging of empty dump trucks going over railway tracks, street traffic, and aircraft overhead.

Jennie rides her bike freely within the bounds of our fence, charging back and forth, and dipping and bucking at the potholes. In quieter moments she enjoys prowling about with a butterfly net after Monarchs and Cabbage butterflies which she draws in her journal. Mourning Doves patrol the gravel to within a couple of metres of our doorway. A fat healthy-looking Woodchuck patrols the fence. House Sparrows and a few ruby House Finches buzz up from weed seeds in the lot, and Ring-bill Gulls keen overhead. All the animals in industrial Toronto seem quite fearless, as if people have long forgotten them in their attention to mechanical things.

Our lot has not been heavily used, and in places the gravel is bound together by low turfy mosses, hiding down below the larger pebbles. One conspicuous species is an almost copper-red velvet, and the other appears to be made up of tiny silver-green carpet loops. Both species are guard-haired

with a dense stand of spore-bearing capsules on fine stalks. Even if this place becomes paved for a parking lot or torn up and hauled away from a building foundation, it will have been a waystation and dispersal source for these tenacious little low-growing plants. Even out in the centre, dwarf mustards grow, little parking lot spirits with wiry stems and small toothy basal leaves.

Our trailer is wedged into the shade of a vigorous Cottonwood. The miniature morning glory, Bindweed, twines delicate Art Nouveau ropes and curls into the rusty chainlink. A hedge-like tangle of Nightshade, lush and dark, presses against the fence, slowly changing its purple flowers into red berries. Flat silvery carpets of Silverweld spread by runners from the shelter of the fence. Tall Evening Primrose flaunts its lemony yellow flowers, and shorter spikes of Vipers Bugloss glow blue and then ripen into prickly grey maturity. The narrow north end of the lot, visited regularly by our venerable Groundhog, pockets into a wilderness of tall Queen Anne's Lace, White Sweet Clover and purple-blooming thistle.

In the meadows a short walk away along Unwin Street at the base of the Leslie Street Spit, bumblebees hang heavily on untidy purple-pink blossoms of knapweed and a Chipping Sparrow "chip-chip-chip's" from the tall tops of a thicket of Sweet Clover misted with white bloom. The grass is full of a high singing – ratchets, creaks and zee's. Dark brown crickets with light brown heads scurry down among the grass roots. I surprise an elfin green Katydid, poised to jump from a bleached white Goldenrod gall, and a pert young grasshopper in a brown and yellow jacket shifts nervously as I peer at it among the stems of this year's Goldenrod. Much of the Goldenrod foliage has been stripped away by little striped chrysomelid beetles, *Trirhabda virgata*, the same beetles that Fred and Lee Ann met on Cherry Beach. They are mating here, the females heavy with eggs. It seems that where the plants are bushy with virus or swollen with stem galls the leaves were less palatable, and the beetle larvae left them alone. Isolated healthy plants and the least-deformed clones are just beginning to bloom, and the few flowers are crowded with Flea Beetles like tiny metallic skipping seeds.

Golden-
rod
with
virus
and
gall

Chrysomelid
beetles mating

Leslie Street Spit, Toronto, 6 August

The Leslie Street Spit, a short block south of camp, is a large area of the lake turned into land by the dumping of excavated material from construction. Made of crushed bits of the city's bones, it began in the 1950s with dumping of rubble, ashes and crushed battery casings, and extended into the lake as a network of causeways of fill hauled from the Yonge Street subway as it was extended north of Eglinton. Still, as Torontonians tear down and rebuild their city, it grows out into the lake, forming bays which are then filled with material too contaminated to be dumped directly into the water. The spit has been gradually colonized by the plants and animals that have filtered through urban Toronto.

The landscape is made up of steep-banked highlands bounded by deep water, with none of the wetlands or isolated ponds that could so easily be made here. In our wanderings we found one Beaver lodge, built on a steep shore, and one remnant pond cut off by rubble fill that looks as if it would be a satisfactory home for newts or frogs, but neither seem to have reached it. It does support Corixid water bugs, flitting through its clear water, and on its sandy bottom matted with *Chara* and filimentous green algae, a big population of European Ear Snail, and a smaller number of juvenile Great Pond Snails.

The end of the spit is a flat gull-loafing lot, marked by its weekday occupants' leavings. Its weekend users are bicyclists and rollerbladers. An artificial drumlin is topped by the stout red and white tower of the navigation light, and the flanks of its hill are yellow-spangled by the aromatic herb Tansy in full bloom. As we found on the Outer Bruce Peninsula, here too Tansy is more abundant farther toward the tip than the otherwise dominant Goldenrod.

We all leave camp at in the evening to see the Cormorant colony. The air becomes lake-fresh and soft with Sweet Clover scent as we pedal south from the gate on the paved roadway. Poplar woods border the road on our right. Beyond fields of Sweet Clover and Goldenrod three earth-movers crouch like bulky yellow dinosaurs resting together, and beyond them the rubble-heaps of their work show whitely against the long ribbon of indigo blue lake. Cottonwood fluff drifts across the road, together with fluttering and sailing Monarch Butterflies.

When we walked in yesterday we found a Monarch resting-place. Glancing into a thicket of young Willows beneath the Poplars, we saw two Willow saplings decked out with broad orange leaves that fluttered, detached and re-attached themselves. There were more

than a hundred on the little trees, with more moving through the woods. Now they aren't here and I am disappointed, as I came prepared to sketch them. Fred says that he saw about 50 feeding on Purple Loosestrife by a steep-banked pond near the tip. This is evidently one wildlife species that appreciates the dreaded marsh invader.

Flowers of *Gaillardia* glow by the path like orange and yellow coals of fire just before we dip down to cross a foot-bridge floating on metal drums. From a large pond, banked with bands of Purple Loosestrife and yellow-flowered Tansy, four young Nightherons rise and flap away ahead of us. As we pause to watch, a Great Blue Heron also lifts from the pond to glide lazily close overhead.

We follow Fred down a track to the Cormorant colony. Bordered by tall grass and overarched by trees, it appears to have been a dying-ground for young Ringbill Gulls. We pass a flattened, dried, feather rag of a carcass every few metres. Then the ground becomes trampled earth as it opens out under cottonwoods, spattered with droppings and littered with sticks and bones and more dead gulls. The air, which had begun to be musty beneath the close trees, now smells brown and fishy and we are surrounded by pattering sounds in the branches of the tall Cottonwoods and plopping noises on the ground. Silvery Alewives are being regurgitated by Cormorants in nests and branches above and all around us, as they lighten their crops in case of emergency. Some young are sooty grey,

but most are fully fledged
and quite black, with
brilliant orange
throats. They
make many
noises, the most
surprising of
which are guttural
roaring grunts. The
Cottonwood twigs
droop, their leaves
mottled white as if by
spray paint. From beyond the
Cormorants we hear the voices of gulls
and radio noise from boats in the bay.

King's Mill Park, Etobicoke, 9 August
We returned to King's Mill Park to
sketch the lawn and the treed bank
above the valley slope. Fred posed with
Jennie on a blanket for a few minutes,
and then, while I inked in the back-
ground, he cycled off to describe the
bicycle route down the Humber River
and east along the waterfront and harbour, back to our Leslie Street camp.

He took the long undulating drive
up to Stephen Road, and then passed
through a neighbourhood of apartment
buildings to the steep downward path
into Humber River Park, which is a
band of lawn wrapped around a sewage
treatment plant. The path runs down
through woods of Manitoba Maple and
orange-flowered Jewelweed, to lawn
parks, past the tall phalanxes of hybrid
Cattail that line the Humber River.

As it comes out of the south Humber Park the trail runs in fenced kinks
to pass under the Queensway bridge
and then curls around to cross the

Humber on the
Queensway bridge
sidewalk. Fred found
getting there by bike much
more direct than our canoe route had
been. He followed the bike route under
CN and Gardiner Expressway bridges,
whose I-beams were lined with Pigeons
and floored with their accumulated
droppings, old nests and dead young,
and came out on the north side of
Lakeshore Boulevard.

The trail crosses Lakeshore at
Wildermere Avenue, where cyclists ig-
nore signs to dismount before crossing,
and then runs along Sunnyside Beach.
Fred threw scraps of Grapefruit peel to
mobs of screaming young Ringbill
Gulls who collided like rugby players
for the chance to catch and reject the
peels, while adult gulls stood well away
from the melee. One juvenile was lame
with a deformed foot and a Canadian
Wildlife Service band on the other
ankle.

Starlings waddled in flocks, pecking

into the short pale grass. Canada Geese stood grazing while Pigeons wandered the lawn, and insect-catching Barn Swallows sliced the air overhead. A steady stream of cyclists, joggers and rollerbladers moved in both directions along the smooth asphalt path, a human parallel to the perpetual motion of the stream of fuming steel and rubber that rushed close at hand along Lakeshore Boulevard, and again inland, higher and faster, along the Gardiner Expressway.

The trail proceeded along a strip of lawn between traffic and parking lots, to what Fred recorded as an inexplicably ugly monument to Sir Casimir Gzowski (1813-1898). Arriving at Lakeshore Parklands, Fred reflected that through decades of driving past on Lakeshore Boulevard he had always been attracted to this crescent sand beach behind breakwaters and a bay of moored sailboats. Now he was here, and signs warned: "Polluted Water – Swim at Your Own Risk," and "If you find a needle do not touch it! Tell a life guard or Parks Attendant." These officials were absent, but sure enough, there was an insulin syringe in the drift, which was made up of goose-pulled Waterweed and all kinds of plastic, especially waterworn styrofoam. He thought it ought to be a good spring drift site though, if there are any land snails to be washed into the lake there.

The trail swings up onto a rise around some lakeshore buildings and a parking lot above the crayfish collection site of our canoe trip, and then down through a parkland a little away from both traffic and lake, through plantings of Austrian Pine. Then it runs as the side lane of a paved road and along a seawall toward Ontario Place, around which Fred detoured, following a route marked by painted stripes on the pavement (blue eastbound, green westbound), and runs inland of the docks of heavy-bodied motor cruisers and the moored destroyer. At the flower bed along the causeway to Ontario Place, he paused to take note of a cheerful array of feral garden flowers and weeds.

After cycling through a lawn-park beside the embankments where sailboats are moored at anchor, Fred passed the elegant white Acanthus facade of Tip Top Tailors. The route then went inland along Lakeshore, to the south end of Spadina Avenue, where a dozen Austrian Pines grow in pots. He continued under the spans of the

Gardiner Expressway, past the base of the CN Tower, and a steady stream of people evidently walking to a Blue Jays baseball game. Continuing to pedal eastward under the shelter of the Gardiner Expressway, Fred passed parking lots and tall tan buildings to the odour of meat vendors serving the baseball crowds. Some buildings are also indoor parking lots, and at the base of one of these a small garden bed supports a fairly prosperous-looking crop of sweet Corn.

York Street took him south to Queen's Quay West, where between the street and sidewalk, thornless Honey Locusts and Ashes are planted in earthen spaces in the brick and concrete, growing healthy and green in a canyon of tall buildings, where clusters of People wait for buses.

Farther east the office buildings and shopfronts give way to big open parking lots and the industrial buildings of the harbour. The bicycle lane ends at Lakeshore Road, and the trail then runs on the gravelly CN right of way to Cherry Street, where salt-crusted soil under the Gardiner Expressway reminded Fred of the crusty alkali of Alberta sloughs.

Continuing toward camp via Cherry Beach and the bikeway, he followed the marked bike trail which runs through open Cottonwood groves on lakeside fill. This was the first substantial length of trail explicitly made as a bike route, but it dumped him out on the Bailey bridge over the R.L. Hearn Generating Station cooling water inlet with no explanation of how to cover the kilometre to the rest of the trail on Leslie Street. It seemed that the Martin Goodman Trail was not marked where the standards of existing roads didn't meet certain specifications, leaving cyclists to find their own route between sections of approved trail.

Port of Toronto, 11 August

Jennie painted a Monarch caterpillar today, which she found on Milkweed in our camp parking lot. She is keeping it in my glass painting box to watch it munch Milkweed leaves and change into a chrysalis. On the morning of 14 August it had eaten all but a scrap of the Milkweed she had given it and went up to the top of the glass box, where it wove a sparse silk pad. By afternoon it was hanging from the centre of this pad. She drew it again at this stage, but it died, and maggot-like larvae, perhaps parasitoids, emerged from it and went off to pupate themselves and perhaps emerge as parasitic wasps, tiny and elegant.

Early this afternoon Lee Ann bike-toured around the block of our industrial neighbourhood. Heading west on Commissioners from the corner of Leslie Street, she passed between Dufferin Cement & Concrete and our noisy neighbour International Iron and Metal, and took note of a majestic Horse Chestnut tree and rows of dusty-leaved young Cottonwoods and White Poplars. A constant roaring convoy of heavy trucks shook the ground and threw up dust and diesel fumes.

She cycled past a Canada Post building, a Metro Works yard, and the

Toronto Transit Commission Lakeshore Complex, which holds corralled battalions of Wheel-Trans buses, waiting to do battle with the next day's traffic. Across from the barren chainlinked grounds of LaFarge Canada Inc. and their row of portly cement trucks, she found a small grove of Black Willow and Manitoba Maple gracing the grounds of a construction supplier.

Across the shipping channel, where a few old yachts and fishing boats await paint and repairs, is a barren field set about with big blue plastic barrels. There, languidly grazing the short sparse grass were about 20 Canada Geese. Among them rested about 30 Ringbill Gulls, and swinging in the chainlink fence, in all the attitudes of a circus act, perched three young Grackles and five or six Starlings: street birds, hanging out. Farther down the fence, lined with Cottonwood, Manitoba Maple and Austrian Pine, Lee Ann read a sign announcing that this is the decommissioned site of the Shell Canada Toronto Plant.

A lake freighter was docked, awaiting cargo from the huge Paperboard Industries Corporation that sprawls on both sides of the road, one lot full of trailers, another with huge stacks of crushed-for-recycling heavy paper products.

About halfway down this street Lee Ann found the "Commissioners Recycling Facility for Blue Box Material Recovery." Its turn-of-the-century red brick walls set with large shadowy many-paned windows inspired her sense of history.

The lot of Teperman New and Used Building Supplies was filled with balls of scrap cable and wire, old exhaust pipes and chimney chutes, and farther down, a concrete floor lined with White Poplars is turning wild, growing Cattails and Goldenrod in its cracks. Beyond it, steep grassy berms partially hide a farm of huge fuel storage tanks. Lee Ann passed QUNO Recycling Corp. as she approached Cherry Street, and a demolition site labelled Denlan Environmental Group, which was "dusting and noising away." Closer to the corner, she passed a long row of Catalpa trees, their snake-bean seedpods slithering down below long bright leaves in the half sun of the afternoon.

By late afternoon the air is oppressive and threatening. A small-winged long-abdomened wasp, which Joyce Cook later identified for us as *Pelecinus polyturator*, came into camp. These wasps parasitize larval June Beetles which they find by probing the soil with their long abdomens. We watch a dark grey pall roll in from the north, an ominous cloud bank with a yellowish pink glow beneath, and everyone is lethargic or agitated. I can't settle to any kind of work, and pack distractedly for a bicycle trip, delaying my departure until its already too late to leave. I can't even sit down and think, caught between "fight and flight." The air has been bad all day, and by the look of the sky, will become worse yet, so we decide to break camp and move to Scarborough.

8

Park Street Camp

Park Street, Scarborough, 18 August
We are camped on a little driveway in
Scarborough, in a community so
densely settled that the area occupied
by the tiny houses perceptibly reduces
the density of trees, compared with the
other residential areas we have sur-
veyed. A big multi-branched Sunflower
sprawls in the gravelly garden bed behind the house with a Monarch flexing
its wings as it sucks nectar from one of
the 23 sun-following blooms. After the
Monarch's turn, a worn-down old
Honey Bee worker, a Yellowjacket
wasp, a Greenbottle Fly, a Cabbage
Butterfly and a green-backed solitary
Bee come to the blooms. Dogday Cicadas whine from somewhere in the trees.

The backyard is almost fully occupied by a double-trunked Norway Maple with a horizontal limb for Jennie's
swing, a 5-m Crabapple tree with
twisted trunks and the trunk of a hand-
some Red Maple that was evidently
killed by the flooded yard freezing in
last winter's long hard cold. Two small
metal sheds, plastic composters, and a
dwarf Apple tree bearing a few fruit
complete the backyard retinue. This
lawn has a few dicot weeds, a major
sign of environmental health to us, but
the ultra-neat yard of the neighbour
has none.

We spread plant press blotters out to
dry beneath the patio awning and sit
on its brick planter wall, Jennie drawing a Cicada in her journal, Fred taking
notes and Lee Ann entering data into
the computer, while I paint plants beneath an umbrella out in the yard. The
trailer is backed up snugly against the
house wall and a blue-tarp-covered an-
tique car. Last night we heard a Raccoon rifling our under-trailer vegetable
stores.

**Glen Stewart Ravine, Toronto,
19 August**
Running south from Kingston Road to
Queen Street, this fragment of natural
ravine, is a tiny island of woodland,
surrounded and fenced on all sides by
houses and roads. To the north and
south of Glen Stewart Ravine, its creek
runs unseen underground in pipes and
culverts. Here, where the ravine is
deeper and broader, the creek surfaces
to run through a remnant of its origi-
nal forest. Although the muddy banks
are extensively eroded, in places they
are untrampled enough to grow Solomon's Seal, Wild Ginger and *Clintonia*
lilies.

This evening Lee Ann entered the
southeast end of the Ravine from a
small residential street north of Queen,
on a footpath past a slope of young
Sumac and full-crowned Sugar Maples.

On her left, an unmowed grassy bank sloped down to a little sand-bottomed stream flowing away into a small culvert. A Mulberry tree with dark shiny leaves overhung the streamlet, shading a rich cover of Jewelweed and Coltsfoot. The steep bank rose to a tall stand of old Red Oaks and finally to Glen Manor Drive winding along the western brink of the ravine.

She was delighted to find plaques along the path, labelling particular species of trees: *Acer rubrum* (Red Maple), *Tsuga canadensis* (Hemlock), *Betula alleghaniensis* (Yellow Birch), one of which had been cut down, its old stump rotting away. She found bushes of her new friend Witch Hazel beneath the long stretching limbs of an old Beech and an even taller and older-looking Red Oak.

N a comfortable bench beneath another Red Oak, Lee Ann sat to write about the creek, winding between banks of thick, heavy mud, fallen away with the sharp curves in its course, and dug into deep holes by Dogs. Severe bank erosion, cutting a gully in the east slope, had claimed one Manitoba Maple, and bared the roots of six others.

She became aware of a constant variety of Dog noises, barks and yelps and yowls from all directions. The park has an area where Dogs can run unleashed. Trumpet-barking heralded a Dog parade, long before it rounded the bend in into sight. Three Dogs chased each other through the creek, bouncing and jumping like clowns. Four Basset Hounds beguiled a black Dog with long, white whiskers. The attending audience walked just behind and nearly in step, talking to one another about the weather.

At first the ground was very clear, "picked clean of debris." When she began to find natural forest floor litter beneath the Oak and Maple trees, Lee Ann turned several sticks and logs on the slope of a muddy gully, uncovering rich black soil, trundling armadillo-like sowbugs and an active, shiny black Ground Beetle, but only one worm, and no salamanders.

Up a tall flight of stairs on the east slope of the ravine, she entered a dusk-shadowed woods, glowing with ghostly Paper Birches. She held a mosquito buzzing in her hand, the first since Grindstone Creek, and realized how few of these one meets in the city. The thick-stemmed, jointed *Polygonum cuspidatum*, Japanese Knotweed, which Lee Ann calls Bamboo Weed, spread its continuous understorey along the stairway from its beds at the bottom of the ravine.

A path leading away from the stairs at the top soon met a paved sidewalk coming in from the street. At a fence guarding houses and back yards, a footpath led her down into the ravine again, this time under a heavy canopy of Maple, Oak and Paper Birch. She continued north along the main stream course under Manitoba Maples and Black Willows, to the watery notes of the creek. Sounds of People and their Dogs had suddenly ceased, leaving the ravine to the approaching darkness.

Following the creek upstream, she

found it flowing in a deep gully, full of bits of logs and scattered leaf litter. Soon it was joined by another from the side, which was crossed by a foot bridge. It became difficult to identify trees in the falling dusk. By the glow of her headlamp and by leaf silhouette against the fading sky, she found an Ash tree. Oaks seemed to make up two thirds of the upper canopy and Beech most of the rest. The mid-canopy was mostly Maple, Cherry, and Witch Hazel.

Continuing past two more inflowing streams and crossing a plank boardwalk over the creek, slipping among the long arms of a pair of strong-trunked oaks and then along a path closely overhung by trees, she finally arrived at the wooden stairway to Kingston Road at the north end of the park. The soft chirruping of crickets signalled that it was time to go; Venus was already brightly twinkling and the last walker had said goodnight.

Leslie Street to Bluffers Park, Metro Toronto, 12 August

Today began overcast, but with no rain, and Jennie and I drove Fred and Lee Ann with their bicycles back to the Leslie Street parking lot, leaving them to work eastward to Bluffers Park, where we plan to rendezvous at sunset.

They started north on the Martin Goodman Trail along Leslie Street, and ran into intense smog at the spiral exit of the end of the Gardiner Expressway. With fumes from the sewage treatment plant the air was "thick enough to cut" in spite of a strong cool wind.

The trail swept them along Lake-shore Road, past the fenced-off lawns of the Main Treatment Plant, cropped by Canada Geese and pecked by Starlings, then along a narrow asphalt path, past lawns of Weeping Willows, Sycamore Maple and Austrian Pine.

Sitting under Poplars and Willows in Ashbridge's Bay Park, they watched a Solitary Sandpiper pecking along the goose-tracked waterline, tweaking and bobbing with toy-like precision. Lee Ann counted 16 Mallards preening by the water's edge, 13 Geese on the close-cropped lawn, and one Ringbill Gull dead by its fellow, who "doesn't know that it's waiting to die."

They biked through the park to the southwest point where heavy rounded limestone boulders range like a fortress along the outer headland. A stiff south-easterly breeze drove the lake into a chop, which sloshed milky green, among the boulders. Terns were having a hard time fishing, most of their dives ending in graceful up-swoops about a metre from the surface. They looked like Arctic Terns, as their bills appeared to have no dark tip. Some terns at a beach farther back on the east side were having more success catching several silvery fish. A sailboat picked up speed with successive corrections to the set of its sails until it caught the wind abeam and rounded the point close inshore. A tugboat heading east towed a barge heaped with a mountain range of gravel piles; windsurfers fly up alone close inshore.

Fred and Lee Ann continued through beachside public land along paved paths and boardwalks to the

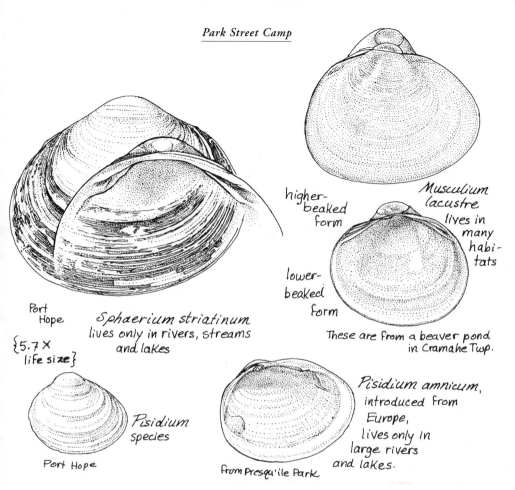

higher-beaked form

lower-beaked form

Musculium lacustre lives in many habitats

These are from a beaver pond in Cramahe Twp.

Port Hope

Sphaerium striatinum lives only in rivers, streams and lakes

{5.7 × life size}

Pisidium species

Port Hope

Pisidium amnicum, introduced from Europe, lives only in large rivers and lakes.

from Presqu'ile Park

shallow bay of Woodbine Beach, with its tennis courts, raked sand, beached rescue rowboats, and lifeguards in welded pipe towers. The stiff onshore wind drove a low surf into the bay. No one was swimming. There were a few Sandpipers and many Ringbill Gulls, some of them carrying what looked like empty matchbooks in their bills.

The beach broadens across from Kew Gardens, a lawn-park with large trees and vivid flowerbeds. Offshore lie turtle-shaped groynes of large stones. Past Kew Gardens the trail continues along the beach, on boardwalk and bike trail, where the construction of

detention tanks for the combined sanitary and storm sewer system was almost complete.

The marked trail ended at Balmy Beach, a narrow sandy beach-park through a residential area, with more "turtle groynes" forming tombolos offshore.

A little farther and they entered Scarborough, arriving at the R.C. Harris Filtration Plant, a gracious Art Deco building, where they took a steep winding road down to the parking lot, and saw many Dogs with people on leashes. Fred climbed down to look for drift, past a work area where the filtra-

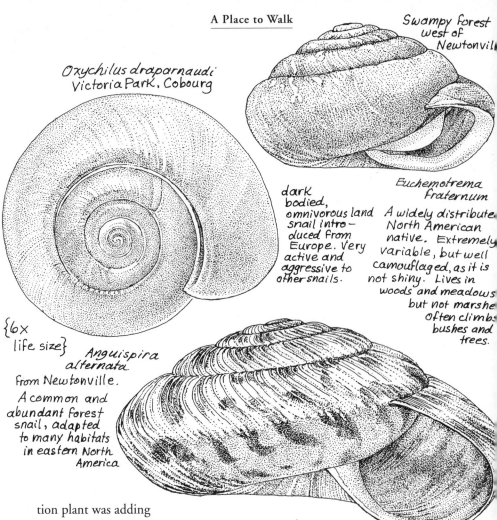

Swampy forest
west of
Newtonvil[l]

Oxychilus draparnaudi
Victoria Park, Cobourg

Euchemotrema
fraternum

dark
bodied,
omnivorous land
snail intro-
duced from
Europe. Very
active and
aggressive to
other snails.

A widely distribute[d]
North American
native. Extremely
variable, but well
camouflaged, as it is
not shiny. Lives in
woods and meadows
but not marshe[s]
Often climb[s]
bushes and
trees.

{6x
life size}
Anguispira
alternata
from Newtonville.

A common and
abundant forest
snail, adapted
to many habitats
in eastern North
America

tion plant was adding some type of Zebra Mussel control. He found no snails or crayfish parts in the line of feathers, twigs and leaves at water's edge.

East of the filtration plant, Fallingbrook Road plunges into a ravine close-set with Tudor style houses along stone curbs, shaded by Silver Maple and Red Oak. They turned up Fallingbrook Avenue past younger, less imposing houses and concrete curbs, to Kingston Road with its close-packed houses, stream of cars and, farther east, the fenced-in preserve of the Toronto Hunt Club.

Its fence was engulfed in a green wall of little Siberian Elms, farther on by tangled blankets of Grape and Virginia Creeper vines, and then *Smilax*'s broad round leaves below the grape. Wanting to see the lake again, they coasted south down Warden Avenue, past more houses to its end, at the brink of the bluff where a steep path runs down the loose clay bank. A party of young People were noisily daring each other to descend it.

Through a gap in the trees, Fred and

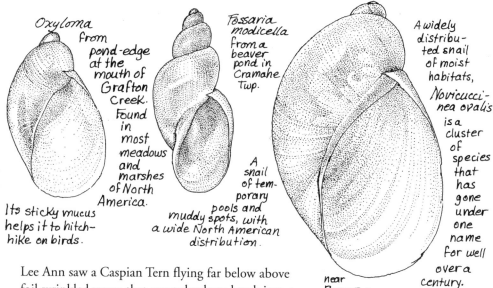

Oxyloma from pond-edge at the mouth of Grafton Creek. Found in most meadows and marshes of North America. Its sticky mucus helps it to hitch-hike on birds.

Fossaria modicella from a beaver pond in Cramahe Twp. A snail of temporary pools and muddy spots, with a wide North American distribution.

A widely distributed snail of moist habitats, *Novicuccinea ovalis* is a cluster of species that has gone under one name for well over a century. near Borers Falls.

Lee Ann saw a Caspian Tern flying far below above foil-wrinkled waves that crept slowly to break into a tracery of foam on a thin curve of shore. Blending in the distance with the haze of the sky, the lake seemed so large it could be the ocean. A lone Monarch, flitting on white fairy flowers of Wild Cucumber, flew up and inland.

Then they came up Harding Avenue to Kingston Road and cycled east to Rosetta McLain Park, where big flocks of Bank Swallows swept and darted about the bluff edge and over the lake. Brick paths coursed through the park, through concentric beds of vibrantly coloured cultivated flowering herbs and around a couple of massive granite erratics (one with water pumped over its surface like a waterfall). At the edge of the bluff they met a few twisted old White Spruce trees, native elders looking over Lake Ontario with aged dignity, as Sitka Spruce look over Hecate Strait on the West Coast of B.C.

By following streets along the bluff, Fred and Lee Ann soon found themselves in Scarborough Heights Park, a modest parkette, where grapevines draped over the trees below the edge of the bluff. Much of the bluff

{5.5 – 6.5 × life size}

Stagnicola elodes, from a beach pond near Carr Marsh. Abundant in all kinds of aquatic habitats, especially thick vegetation and muddy bottoms, throughout Canada and the Northern USA.

77

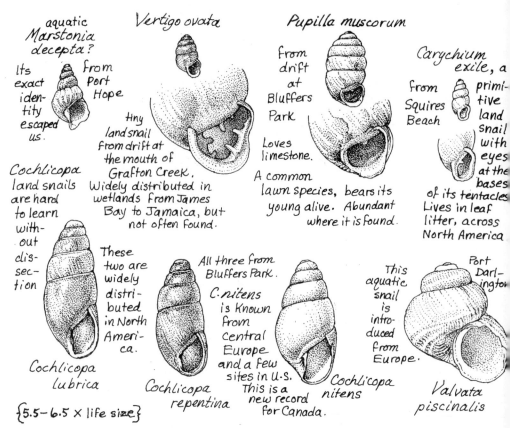

aquatic *Marstonia decepta?*
Its exact identity escaped us.
from Port Hope

Vertigo ovata
Tiny land snail from drift at the mouth of Grafton Creek. Widely distributed in wetlands from James Bay to Jamaica, but not often found.

Pupilla muscorum
from drift at Bluffers Park
Loves limestone.
A common lawn species, bears its young alive. Abundant where it is found.

Carychium exile, a primitive land snail with eyes at the bases of its tentacles
from Squires Beach
Lives in leaf litter, across North America

Cochlicopa land snails are hard to learn without dissection

These two are widely distributed in North America.

Cochlicopa lubrica

All three from Bluffers Park.
C. nitens is known from central Europe and a few sites in U.S. This is a new record for Canada.

Cochlicopa repentina

This aquatic snail is introduced from Europe.

Cochlicopa nitens

Port Darlington

Valvata piscinalis

{5.5 – 6.5 × life size}

edge in that part of Scarborough is taken up by little parks, perhaps to buffer private property from the impermanence of the eroding edges.

They cycled past fenced-in tennis courts into Scarborough Bluffs Park, whose flat lawn comes up to a low cable strung between stout wooden posts. Beyond, the ground breaks away into loess-like ridges and valleys, and there, as surprising as if they had just risen up that moment, stand the Needles, tall slender hoodoos, castellate shapes carved in ashy tan silt by wind and rain from the vertical ribs of the eroding bluff. When Fred and Lee Ann arrived, five Crows accented the starkness of

the tallest form, perched in various attitudes on its head and shoulder and along the curving ridge that still connects it to the bank.

On the west side they looked out to a lush wild view of the bluffs, only modified by a few houses peeking through the woods, a low revetment roadway along the lake, and a dredge working for the filtration plant, far out on the lake.

Bluffers Park lay below, a broad flat of land where lake once lay, as if a road had come down the bluff and flowed out into a big delta of drives, bays, paths and lawns, decorated with streetlights, pavilions and marina. There was movement too, far below –

Valvata perdepressa

Only shells of this aquatic snail have ever been found, frequently abundant on shores. No-one knows where the live ones hide.

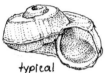

Port Hope

typical   reduced carina

Valvata tricarinata

This aquatic snail loves to live on water plants.

A temporary pool species, this snail lives where there is plenty of calcium carbonate and shade. Teeth inside the shell may protect it from predators.

Hawaiia minuscula

above Borers Falls

A North American land snail, that has travelled the world as many European snails are known to do.

likes gardens

Planorbula armigera from Port Darlington

{5.5 X life size}

Discus rotundatus, a land snail. Found in Bluffers Park drift.

Introduced from Europe, they are widely scattered but rare.

cars, boats, soccer players, picnickers. Fred picked out our red truck in one of the lots, so Lee Ann went over the edge to meet us, while he stayed with the bikes and watched birds and People.

Descending the bluffs, Lee Ann found that the dusty clay pillars and edges reminded her of places she'd known in Australia. She took a worn path down to the narrow top edge of a "finger" which she balanced along for a little and then slid down to a lower path. From there she looked down on herons standing hunched and still in the lagoon. She continued down a steep gully bushy with willow, Dogwood and young Paper Birch,

from Port Darlington drift, A native, blind burrowing landsnail

Helicodiscus parallelus

Vallonia costata Bluffers Park
both common in city lawns and mountaintops worldwide.

Vallonia pulchella

with lots of Queen Anne's Lace and Goldenrod. Near the bottom, the clay turned wet and slippery. Pushing through a thicket of tall White Sweet Clover about the margin of the pond, she heard the din of a soccer game across the lagoon.

Jennie and I had arrived at Bluffers around supper time to paint the view looking east along the bluffs. We found a vantage point on an armoured bar of land beyond the marina. This spring Jennie painted an oil of the distinctive shapes of the Needles, looking west from the parking lot, but this evening the sky in the northwest glared too brightly for me to look in that direction, so I turned the other way, painting the warm tones of the bluff's exposed flanks as they stretched into blue haze along the lake. In contrast with the close bustling city, I find the distant bluffs as majestic as the Rocky Mountains.

After two hours of painting we met Lee Ann on our way back to the truck. Up the steep winding road out of Bluffers Park, we zigzagged through the dusk along short bluff-top streets to find Fred waiting in Scarborough Bluffs Park. As he waited, he wrote about the grating of Common Terns, the rollicking harsh "kirk-a-dee-ah" of Caspians, the twittering of swallows, the notes of passing gulls and a few Goose calls. As dusk fell the birds tightened their flocks around roosting areas, Geese at the outflow from the lagoon, gulls on the bar and ducks in the lagoon. The crescent moon showed high in the west, and the sunset was leaving a diffuse pink glow in the north, when suddenly the lights down at Bluffers Park become its most conspicuous feature.

Scarborough Bluffs Park, 14 August
In the late afternoon we revisit the Needles. I sit on the grassy brink to draw them in ink, with Bluffers Park showing down below, while Fred and Jennie help a man and a boy who were trying to fly a kite. The treetops are tossing and streaming, but they shelter the park from the offshore winds. Clouds sail past in procession, all canted up like speedboats. A wedge of moon rises, steady and translucent against the blue.

Stepping over the guard rail, we walk along to the tip of this facet of the eroded bluffs and a flank of pale clay faces us, wrinkled with tiny grooves cut by the rain. Clinging to the "prow," a group of young Aspen protect their little bit of the bluff. Someday they will be undercut during a storm to fall away in a big chunk of roots and clay. The other side of that leaf of land is lightly wiry with little sumacs, their foliage beginning to redden. Autumn may begin in August under difficult living conditions. A knot of Willows at the edge of the bank is nearly completely undercut, their naked roots hanging down. A fringe of Chicory plants leans out at the very brink as if they really would rather fly.

Wetlands are usually flat, but here a stand of cattails runs down a damp slope like a green slash for about 30 m. Those at the top are Broadleaf Cattails,

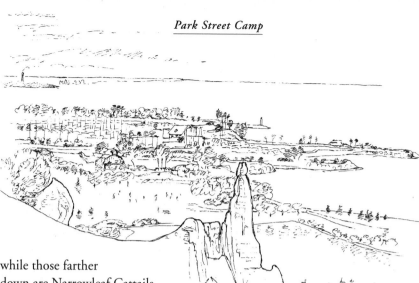

while those farther
down are Narrowleaf Cattails,
with no hybrids.

As we sit on the edge of the
bluff the wind chills us through
sweaters, though it is not cold, and
below us it drives wave arcs against
the beach bar that closes the lagoon
where this spring we found drift
rich with tiny pupillid snails. We
watch the drama, tiny so far below,
of a Dog chasing geese across the
shallow water of the bay. Across from
the last bluffs to the east, past the
Rouge River, lies the Pickering nuclear
plant, then the dark low shoreline at
Squires Beach and Lynde Shores,
then finally Oshawa twinkling in
the dusk.

Bluffers Park to Bellamy Ravine, Scarborough, 15 August

From the easternmost parking lot of
Bluffer's Park, Fred and Lee Ann set
out on foot along a flat sand beach under clearing blue sky with a southwest-
erly breeze.

Where the beach narrowed, close
below the bluffs, they collected a sample of beach drift with land snail shells,
and decided it would be a rich place for
drift in the spring. Narrow-leaved
Willows inhabit the terrace just above
the beach, and above them, a broader-
leaved species, and above them, Coltsfoot, the most widespread herb on the
faces of the bluffs. Most steep slopes
that aren't quite vertical bear a blanket-
ing bed of large round Coltsfoot leaves.
Even on some vertical faces, it chooses
certain strata into which it can work its
roots to create horizontal "hanging gardens."

At the end of the sand beach, our
expeditionaries stood on rocky pebbles,
with the bluffs towering 95 m above

their heads with Sumac, Poplar and Paper Birch at the top.

The bluff retreats by massive slumps that fan out toward the beach. This gradual subsidence fills the little rivulets with so much fine silty sand that they look like potter's slip. Fred and Lee Ann stopped to describe a streamlet several centimetres wide that was cutting a canyon in an alluvial fan of coarse gravel and clay, and spreading its own fan of finer sediment out to the water's edge. They noticed that the water flow wasn't constant, but came in flushing pulses, so Fred climbed up to find out why.

He found that the little stream begins as a spring at the base of the sandy dune layer. It trickles down over newly collapsed masses of clayey till, which it washes into itself, until pregnant with soil it flows rolling down like heavy slow volcanic lava. The advancing liquid finger of sandy clay thickens until it dams itself up. Water that gathers behind it soon breaks through, gradually picking up speed and volume as it erodes away obstacles until it picks up enough clay to slow it down again, beginning another dam forming and breaking cycle. He saw two of these episodes, about 15 minutes apart. At the bottom, Lee Ann looked up from her notes just in time to see "a big glug of heavy mud rolling its way slowly down the mud paths." When she put her hand into the mud it was lighter and sandier than she had expected. It was exciting to watch water "digesting" the bluffs so conspicuously into the lake.

Gurgling like underground rivers, these rivulets carve gullies deep into the flanks of the bluff. A much greater flow of water and sediment a month or more ago carried three Sugar Maples down from the brink, flaking a cirque-shaped facet in the bluff edge, and bending down bushes and herbs all the way to the lake. Lee Ann noted that the willows were beginning to turn up from their flattened positions.

A sparse stand of the tall-plumed reed, *Phragmites*, was growing in company with Cattails far up the nearly vertical slope of a seeping clayey bluff face. Above the "vertical wetland," they counted small black holes in a wall of sand, a close community of 50 Bank Swallow burrows, and the larger and more isolated openings of 10 Kingfisher nests.

After climbing high up over a fresh slide to get past its soft, sticky base, they found a narrow gully in the eroding clayey face of the bluffs, now 65 m

Looking east from Bluffers Park

high, banded with narrow hanging gardens of Horsetail and Coltsfoot.

A little farther along the foot of the bluff, the vegetation is laid out in diagrammatic patches, and they collected specimens of some of the dominant species. The Heartleaf Willow, *Salix cordata*, is the most common shrub along the bluff's foot. It bears silky spindle-shaped cabbage galls at the tips of some of its twigs. Barnyard Grass grew in green turves at the bottom and up the face. Evening Primrose, in bloom and very bushy, was common in patches at the bluff foot, and also Pale Smartweed with pink caterpillar catkin blooms. Lance-leaved Goldenrod bloomed in soft billowy patches, and Annual Wormwood was there too, in spots, but not in bloom. Fred was impressed by a small stand of Lambsquarters, 2.5 m tall with a thick woody stem and lush dark green foliage. They harvested branch-tips from this enormous plant and when we cooked them up at camp, we found them mild and succulent for so late in the season.

Within a kilometre of their Bellamy Creek destination, the bluffs were 60 m high at an "old and glorious" gully, rich and full, like a piece of rainforest. Above the Basswood tree at the bottom, Cattails and *Phragmites* reeds wind their way up the slope, and maples edge the top. They gathered land snail fossils which may have fallen with crumbs of the clayey silt below the root-overhang at the bottom of the bluff, and searched unsuccessfully for more fossils in chunks that had fallen

from the higher bluff, peeling apart blue, grey, green and brown layers of sandy clay.

Fred picked up one *Cambarus* crayfish carapace and a leg. This find started them searching for more drift and they found a few land snails and a Woodchuck jaw where the beach ends at the armoured mouth of Bellamy Creek. There they found an avalanche chute of fallen leaves, branches and other garden waste running down the bluff to end in the lake. Caspian Terns were plunging for fish, and a Herring Gull winged past.

They followed a path up the bank and climbed down onto a broad stone floor, astonished to find such an industrial-strength floodway on this wild a lakeshore. In some places storm sewer flow increases so dramatically when it rains that streamside vegetation succumbs to massive erosion unless the bed is hardened by stone or concrete. The channel for this creek, which drains an area of no more than 2 square km, is 5 m wide and 2 m deep, and is lined with mattress-sized blocks of limestone. The floodway descends in a series of nearly metre-high steps, to fan out and drop a metre and a half to a swish of green "mermaid's hair" and the lake. Lee Ann describes it as a set of giant's steps disguised as an armoured creekway. Today they found only a trickle of water, partly filling the crevices between the huge stones. Fred turned loose rocks in the pavement, but found no animals.

They started up the channel of the floodway until the height of its steps increased to 1.5 m, when they climbed out and walked up the gravel track that runs along the east side.

Bellamy Creek to Rouge River, Scarborough, 16 August

Lee Ann and I head down the ravine that she and Fred came up yesterday. He and Jennie are taking the canoe down Highland Creek to meet us at its mouth near East Point Park. Along the gravel road down into the ravine, I pick the last few sweet "fruitlets" of Red Raspberry from among tired yellow leaves, and then enter heavy shade beneath mature Maple, Beech and Oak and hear the creek trickling clear among stones at the ravine bottom. A crisp evergreen clump of the leathery Christmas Fern grows near the bottom of the steep wooded slope to the creek. Following the creek along the east bank of its shallow stone channel, I stop to write some notes where it slips over the straight edge of a big stone block and then chatters over a rubble of smaller stones. I find nothing beneath them but gravel, which may indicate that this ravine is too often flooded for animals to live in it, though a flurry of small flies dances above the ripples.

Dry brown leaves skid beneath my

feet over traces of a nylon net laid years ago to help retain the bank. Tufts of Buffalo Grass poke through and sweep down-slope like switches of long straight hair. Black Swallowwort, with broad dark green leaves, sprawls over the bank in a tangle of vines. Its tips twist into a rope fringed with paired pointed pods. I collect some of this to draw, and then climb up to join Lee Ann.

We walk down the gravel trail through the woods until the ravine widens to sunshine and Weeping Willows, where round-leaved Coltsfoot paves the ground between stands of Goldenrod. Lee Ann searches the east bank for salamanders, under Maple, Beech and White Pine on a steep clay slope. She finds active red-brown worms, colonies of flat-backed sow bugs, and one Camel Cricket, hunched and glossy golden-brown, with long antennae (which she later drew in her journal).

Black Swallow-wort

Cynachum nigrum

84

I force my way through bushes and ferns to the steep slope on the east side of the little roadway, and drawing a deep breath beneath the big Maples, meet the many-eyed stare of White Baneberry, or "Doll's eyes." The black-dotted white berries are set off handsomely by thick red stems, crowded together atop a thin green stalk. This forest seems such a wild place, and I would like to explore it, but we have far to go today and haven't yet reached the lake. Picking the Baneberry, I pack it carefully in my vasculum.

The path then curves round the base of a yellow-grassed hillside, dotted with Russian Olives like small silver-green clouds. Black-and-yellow-winged grasshoppers clatter up ahead of us, and a pair of big blue dragonflies mating in a double crescent, courses by. The tall Sweet Clover along the track is busy with bees, the first time we have seen them healthy and abundant since leaving the Royal Botanical Gardens in Dundas.

I look up from taking notes about insects, and there, ahead of us, the mouth of Bellamy Ravine opens in a V to the misty infinity of lake and sky. In the shade of a young Locust tree, Lee Ann supports my palette as I stand to paint the view.

We follow the path down a gentle slope beside the broad, armoured sluiceway

"Doll's eyes"
White Baneberry.

Actaea pachypoda

to the mouth of Bellamy Creek. As the path turns east, we have a splendid view of wild bluffs, banded with bedding stripes and gored by little ravines, all pink in the afternoon sun as it retires into a summer haze along the curve of the lake.

We've clattered a little way along the narrow beach, to sit where the pebbles mound up against the prostrate limbs of a Black Willow. The lake has hollowed a shallow cave beneath the Willow roots and the inner walls are patched with velvety moss. The clay of the low bank is bound together by fine moss, lichen and algae. Its surface is weathered like the grain of old cedar rails, with tiny bolsters of moss cushioned into the cracks. A short curtain of big round Coltsfoot leaves overhangs the lip of the bank, and above, a lush green meadow, with Goldenrod and Cattails rises up the slope to Sumacs crowning against the bright hazy sky.

As we begin our hike eastward between towering bluffs and the lake, we pass Dogwood and red Willow roots stretching straight out, naked, from the eroding bank, their rootlets clotted with clay. Vertical branches shoot up all along their length. Below billows of the fine-leaved Goldenrod *Solidago graminifolia* at the top of the low beach bank, we meet

85

a riotous, wavy-purple-stemmed Cockle-bur, *Xanthium*. Its stem and narrowly maple-shaped leaves feel rough, like shark skin. Wave-rounded mud slides bristle with lush green Horsetail right down to the firm flat footing of the beach, a metre from the wave-washed pebbles.

Bellamy Ravine

Our way along the beach is barred by a tangle of trees and bushes brought down by a fresh slide, and we climb up-slope to get around it. The damp clay is puddingy underfoot, and the mud-encrusted vegetation looks like a waterfall that someone has rather messily sculpted in clay. The chaos of mud, herbs and bushes increases toward the bottom, where Willow branches lie lapping in the lake.

Soon we can see the people-built revetment, white, around the point ahead. Stepping carefully on chunks of wet clay which has crumbled down a rough slot in the bank, we look up into a curved chimney in the cliff. Wet-stained arms of clay bank reach out from the curved sandy back wall. Many black "eyes" of Bank Swallow holes look out from the shadows. Suddenly our eyes catch movement, as wet clay slumps from one of the side walls.

The pattering sound of a little waterfall echoes in the half-cylindrical niche it has carved in the bluff face. A little way along the beach, we notice quicksand washing down a winding miniature canyon from the settled plain of an older slide. It is safer to cross its outflow on the log of a fallen Cottonwood. A group of boys, who had passed us as we stood to write, now climb the high ledges of a damp clay wall. They are stomping down little slides that leave scallops in the ledges.

Farther on, we admire drip-sculptures, where loess-like sediment is trailed, dripped and braided like candle wax down the pale crumbly slope. A sudden dry avalanche of sand drops in a momentary slide from high ledges that are evenly fluted like elements of Greek architecture. Some chunks of hard grey clay, washed out of the bank and into the lake, mush into "potter's clay" as we step on them. Straight-bedded clay of a light brown colour breaks out of the bank in flat-sided blocks and tablets. The drying "leaves" separate, like the pages of a cardboard book. Approaching the revetment, we can see a twisted segment of chainlink fence hung up midway in its fall down the grass-ledged corduroy of a steep slope.

Arriving at the beginning of the revetment, we clamber piles of brick and concrete rubble, to the flat sur-faced limestone blocks that pave the seawall, broadly sloping several meters down to the lapping, algae-waving lake.

Standing on the gravel road of the revetment, we feel very much out in the lake, with a much broader view of

Honey-
suckle,
Lonicera sp.

umns, with Sumac, Willows and Manitoba Maple climbing up between them. The sloping revetment roadway has carried us halfway up the bluffs to meet a paved road coming down, and we walk past parents coaching their two children, who bicycle up and down the slope. The clear water of the lake is 25 m below us, washing over slabs of broken concrete nestled in a matrix of asphalt. Gulls patrol back and forth offshore, or swim, with the pink sun on them, like minute sailboats beyond the shadow of the bluffs.

The upper part of the cliff overhangs, almost a cap-rock of hard clay and gravel, and the road descends to revetment level at a laid limestone wall. We can see East Point, our distant destination. Now the cliff rises again, high above us, and near the top, the bricky rectangle of a house foundation is exposed to view like a fossil in the eroded bluff. The revetment ends a little past this sobering sight, and we pick our way past beach fire charcoal and picnic litter over a rubble of concrete along the water's edge. A bat-

the bluffs than we had while creeping along at their feet. Grasshopper song rises from a dry meadow of tall grasses at the foot of afternoon-shaded cliffs. A long, pond-like ditch begins on our left, with a pleasant array of wetland plants – Arrowhead with spikes of white blossoms, Yellow Pond Lily in bloom and the pale fine flowers of Water Plantain, hazing a little bay. There are no frogs here. If it were Newfoundland, people would bring tadpoles to these places.

At the corner of a short pier built out from the revetment, a solitary Nightheron, hunched into a teardrop shape, watches for fish. Small Terns fly, scolding. The eastern end of our long winding ditch is stone-lined, receiving water through the grating of a storm sewer outlet. Glancing up, we see the top corner of an apartment building above the brow of the cliff. A chainlink fence is exposed through gaps in the trees, and down float the voices of children in evening play.

The cliff is broken here into almost regularly spaced battlement-like col-

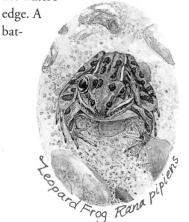

Leopard Frog *Rana pipiens*

tery of swallow nest holes riddles the cliff beyond the west end of Grey Abbey Park.

Now the face becomes dissected by gullies, and between them short spikes of the bluff are tawny-coloured and hairy with bushes. We stop at a deep hazy green pool which receives soapy-smelling water from an arched culvert opening. A giant brick of concrete conglomerate looms up on the pebble beach. It is "conglommed" out of granite stones of many colours, and two broken metal pipes stick mysteriously out of one side.

SONG SPARROW slips among the leafy shoots of old tangled Willow roots at the water's edge. A pleasant sandy walking beach stretches beside a Willowy bank grassed with Horsetail. A big patch of pure Coltsfoot carpets the slope, and the lake is pastel pink and blue. Following a trail over the earthy root wads of leaning Black Willows. We notice tiny bird tracks decorating the mud beneath, with footprints of Raccoon and one vermillion Sumac leaf. The bluff is low now, and from the Sumac jungles across its knees Grape vines creep out to the beach. We pick Lambsquarters tops from plants growing on the first really sandy bank we've seen today, and walk the beach past tracks of barefoot People and Squirrels.

Rounding a low curved flank of bluff we come across a little creek flowing out onto wave-dimpled sand from a green-sloped ravine wooded with Manitoba Maple. This is an idyllic, wild little place to peer into from beneath the boughs

of a leaning tree at its mouth.

Now the bluff slopes gently, clothed with willows and grasses, and we pass a beachside grove of Black Locust trees. Small boulders appear, spaced out by waves along the cobbly shallows. Common Mergansers cruise in a family group close along shore, and a little farther along we count 10 Canada Geese. A grove of tall narrow Black Willows, floored with horsetail gives the impression of a tropical Bamboo brake. Swarming Chironomids cloud at head height over the beach. Even by evening light we can see their big feathery antennae.

The sky is greying and the moon reflects on the water. It is dark enough to make note-taking difficult, and we press on to reach Fred and Jennie. The bluffs are becoming lower and broken between "knees and shoulders," scrubby with Poplar, Willow and Goldenrod. A "stone" half raises its wings and slips into the water, coyly looking back at us with the dark eyes and bill of a Gull. The loose gravel of the beach shifts underfoot, making walking difficult. Reaching East Point, we find that the bluff is no longer smooth and sandy, but coarse and rough with all sizes of gravel. A short bed of close-packed stones is visible about halfway up the nose of the cliff. There is no vegetation between the narrow beach and the bluff here. A crisp edge of turf at the top stands in grassy silhouette against the late evening sky, and ahead the lights of Pickering and Oshawa twinkle like a thin string of diamonds in a dull lilac mist. I write my notes by headlamp.

Shortly after rounding the point I catch a small Leopard Frog as it hops along the edge of a log at the waters edge. Farther on we see another among scrubby Willow bushes near the base of the cliff, but we can't see it well enough to catch it. Later, examining my frog in daylight, I notice that one of its eyes has not developed properly, giving it a permanent squint. Many frog deformities are caused by high toxin levels in the habitat and diet of their parents, and also by contamination of the waters in which they develop as eggs and tadpoles.

Two hundred metres down the beach we come upon a thundering outpouring, which clamours whitely over stones where a culvert issues from a bushy notch in the low bluff. A man approaches the other side as we pick our way across. When we ask whether he has seen Fred and Jennie with the aluminum canoe, we are told that the second fire that we can see glowing far up the dark beach is theirs. We continue, anxiety abated. We signal with our headlamps and promptly they respond.

Now the bluff is no taller than a beach dune. Against the deep velvet blue sky, a glowing orange plume of smoke trails eastward from the top of an incinerator stack. The orange colour must be a reflection of sodium vapour lights on its underside. We pass the first fire, nodding to a group of fire-ruddy youths who greet us and restrain a friendly Dog.

Jennie comes running to greet us, wrapped in Fred's shirt, and we walk together to the fire, where Fred is drying her clothes. Sitting on life jackets, we share the last of our food while hearing the tale of their harrowing trip down Highland Creek from Danforth Park. Jennie later dictated an account of the trip to me: "I helped my Daddy canoe down Highland Creek. It was very difficult. The water was very shallow most of the way. There was big boulders about three inches under the water. When the sun shines on them, it makes the boulders look like they are closer, and it made me frightened that the canoe was going to scrape. I sat on the tip of the bow most of the way, to stable the canoe, and I could see the rocks ahead and help paddle. When the water got shallow, Daddy got out, and I paddled on with Daddy following behind the canoe. Sometimes I helped, jumping with my feet, and when it got too shallow for me I got off the canoe and led it by a rope. One place it was very rocky with big boulders, and Daddy and I had to lift the canoe over into deeper water. Once when we were nearing the lake we saw a big tree lying across the creek ahead. I had to get out and Daddy had to push the canoe underneath some big branches.

"We spent the whole afternoon canoeing down the creek. There are places really slippery with algae, big flat rocks and lumpy with pebbles. I slipped on my hip and my wrist and got all wet, but I was okay. Then when the sun got lower I felt very cold and stopped paddling. Then I started to paddle again when we neared the lake and saw a big break of trees and bushes and wood in the way, but there was a little channel we went in to get out.

"Daddy landed the canoe on the beach and we set off in search of beach wood. There was a lot of it, and mostly dry. A man walked by and said that a Beaver came out at this time every day. He came back a couple of minutes later, with some plastic bait containers and a piece of styrofoam and some beach drift with no snails in it. He put the plastic bait containers in our fire and then lit them for us. Then he said that's the way you light a fire that doesn't have Birch bark. My Daddy wrapped his shirt around me like a dress, and then we dried my clothes by the fire.

"We saw a light at the tip of the beach. We signalled with our head-lamp, short-short-long, and short-long answered back. It was Mommy and Lee Ann."

We decide, with the advice of our neighbours at the other fire, to con-tinue east on the lake to Rouge River Park.

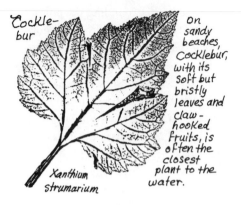

Cockle-bur

On sandy beaches, Cocklebur, with its soft but bristly leaves and claw-hooked fruits, is often the closest plant to the water.

Xanthium strumarium

ALTHOUGH the map shows 4 km between Highland Creek and the mouth of the Rouge, we are under the impression that this will be a quick canoe trip. We are all tired, and it's hard to see whether we're making any progress on the dark water. This time we have only two paddles, one of them the half-sized cedar paddle carved for Jennie by Fred. With each GO train and freight train

that rushes by on the lake-edge tracks, we feel certain that we must be almost there. We strain our eyes to see through low pillows of mist along the beams of our headlamps, and expect that each cluster of lights that flashes between lake edge trees will be the lights of Rouge River Park. Our dark moon-shadows travel solemnly beside us on the silk-smooth water.

It must have taken nearly an hour, moving by faith forward between dark sky and dark water that lifted and fell with the low swells of the sleeping lake. We did finally arrive at the lights of Rouge Beach, paddled past the public washrooms and the Canoe Club, and a little farther yet to round the sandbar at the mouth of the river. Then into the Rouge, as quiet as a pool, reflecting the campfires on its east bank. We dragged the canoe up on the sand, and I huddled down beside a boulder to rest and shelter from the cold breeze, while the others walked to call a taxi. After a long while, they returned with the truck. We loaded the canoe and ar-rived, tired and drowsy with vehicle-warmth, back at the trailer at 01:15.

9

Lynde Shores Camp

Marsh,
beach and bar

Lynde Shores & Cranberry Marsh, Whitby, 22 August

Today we went through a gate from the Lynde Shores Conservation Area parking lot and down a narrow gravel road for over a kilome-tre, until it curved and ran parallel to the beach, past houses and cottages on the north side of the road, to a little lot between two houses, which is to be our home for a week. After positioning the trailer and making supper, we explored a bit.

The beach is soft tan sand, with wave-rows of rounded pebbles higher up, and sorted into fine gravel at the water's edge. The road continues to curve, away from the lake, so we have to walk on the beach to reach the mouth of Cranberry Marsh, now held a few centimetres above lake level by a narrow gravel bar, which People walk across and kayakers attempt to rush over, pushing with their hands. Free now from the city smog, we can enjoy the fresh lake air, but we are not yet free it seems, from the sounds of large machinery, for across the open water of the Lynde Creek, beyond the tall cat-tails and a few marsh-edge trees, a hospital is being built, with swinging cranes, big shovels reaching, and the all-day rumble, moan and clank of machinery.

Grapevines curtain down from the Aspens and Manitoba Maples that face

Alosa pseudo-harengus

Alewife

the lake, and a path runs through the woods of Ash, Poplar, Cedar, Hickory and Willow through the undergrowth of tall Goldenrod. Here a patch of Bedstraw and Vetch thread through fine Buffalo Grass, and there violet leaves spring from beds of dark moss in a special "room" over which Cedar and Beech trees thatch their boughs. Beneath the Willows on the Marsh side, orange-flowered Jewelweed glows behind the border of Cattails. A Leopard Frog leaps from my footstep, and a Harrier, surprised, swings up and across the marsh.

A Chipmunk squeaks sharply, and I head back to camp, pausing to stoop and peer under the large, tired leaves of Mayapple plants, searching for their fruits, like tiny limes, turning yellow and soft as they ripen. The stiff upright stems of Mayapple stand spaced out on a large circular patch of dry earth. As I stand, pondering whether these plants may chemically inhibit other species from growing beneath them, a Shrew darts like a shadow out of, and then back into, the jungle of Strawberry leaves that beds thickly around the perimeter of the Mayapple patch.

Chironomids hover above the beach, swarming in two oval balls, about 70 cm wide and a metre apart, at head-height. I've drawn one here, that had landed on dry sand.

At 21:30, the just-past-full moon shimmers a bright path on the lake, all the way from its shining edge at the indigo sky to the bright crests of the

Chironomid

breaking waves, and then withdraws subtle silk-scarf swirls behind their fine lace edges. In our headlamps we see that the waves have here and there heaped low mounds of multicoloured pebbles that gleam like piles of precious stones. A grey and white Cat scampers ahead of us, in and out of the beams of our lights. The low bluff rises dune-like on our right. Suddenly, in Lee Ann's light, a Toad hops on wet sand, and she catches it. Then we find several more, come down to the lake at night to wet their skins.

Cranberry Marsh, Whitby, 23 August
Lee Ann took a reconnaissance of Cranberry Marsh today, a warm, sunny day with a breeze. She began along the barrier beach, west of our camp, at an old brown cottage under draping Willows. Wild Cucumber with fairy flower spikes, runs all through the Willow, Grape, and Burdock at the beach edge. The undergrowth is thick along the marsh side, and when she tried to walk on the more open marsh edge, she sank in muck to her knees, so she circled the marsh through the woods.

Her route took her through tall jungles of Jewelweed and pushed through Dogwood and Alder thickets. She walked through dense stands of Aster and Goldenrod along an old field, and then back under Willow and Poplar, to see Mayapples in yellow fruit. She found a tall grass-forest of *Phragmites* along the marsh Cattails on the north side. She met many insects along the way: a thick swarm of mothy brown-winged caddisflies on the barrier beach, large mounds attended by big black ants on the old-field side of the marsh-edge woods, and black velvet winged damselflies, blue and red dragonflies, and a yellow-spotted dragonfly that landed on her shoulder.

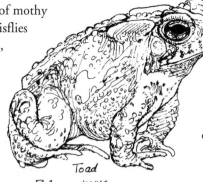

Toad
Bufo americanus

There were Canada Geese, Mallards, "White Swans," sandpipers, Great Blue Herons and a Nightheron in the marsh, and Raccoon tracks under an old Willow. She visited three wooden viewing platforms on the west, north and northeast sides, which people reach on gravel paths from roads, where birders watch for hawks during fall migration. Lee Ann came back to camp along the Eastbourne Beach Road, burdened with plastic bags of the plants she is learning to know and vials of snail shells – *Stagnicola elodes* from a dried marsh, with some *Oxyloma cf retusa*, spring annuals, that would have oviposited and died by mid-July – and pages of notes, tired limbs and wet boots.

Mouth of Lynde Creek, Whitby, 23 August

A grey cloud of little fish drifts along the murky marsh edge of the narrow gravel bar, just a metre from the repeating rush of the cold lake wavelets. The cloud rises, seething with individual fish bodies like a living stream with currents and eddies, each fish only a centimetre or less from its neighbours. I think they must tickle each other's sides with their pushing and passing. Occasionally a spark of light is struck as one flashes sideways. Up along the sun-warmed shallows they swarm. Some turn on their sides to wriggle over a tattered drifted Pond Lily leaf, and their silver sides shine bright blue from the sky. They are deep-bodied little fish, I can see, each with a black spot behind the gill cover. They seem to have a light blue spot on the top of their heads – its hard to see as they all flow so fast. I'd like to be down there with them, roiling together in the warm water. Fred catches a few and we see that they are Alewives, and we think they must soon leave the warm water of the marsh for the deep cold water of the lake.

Lee Ann saw six Great Blue Herons and several Nightherons vying for choice positions near the bar here yesterday evening. A challenger would approach one closer to the bar with head down and wings held out in a "monstrous" cape, usually being met by the defender in a similar attitude. One Great Blue that held the bar itself stood very tall and still, with beak tilted upward. Were they waiting for the Alewives to make their exodus to the lake by night? The little fish certainly did not seem ready to enter the lake during daylight, even when Fred opened a temporary gap in the bar to entice them.

ROUGE RIVER

Scarborough, 27 August
We put the canoe in at Glen Rouge Park today, just a little upstream of the Hwy 2 bridge, below a broken concrete weir. The almost-clear creek threads past sand and gravel bars, between grassy banks of clay and tumbled-in boulders and rocks. Before embarking, we turn stones to find several of the introduced crayfish *Orconectes rusticus*, one of them a real monster, with claws about 4 cm long. It creeps backward on the short grass bank where the net has dumped it, until Fred can grasp its carapace, safe from the terrible claws. There are no native crayfish here.

Raccoon tracks pattern the mud of the oak-shaded bank, and Honey Bees lick up moisture near the water's edge. I record an air temperature of 25°C and water temp of 21°C as I fill out a data sheet for the crayfish specimens, and we push off at 13:00 hr. We soon have to get out again to pull the canoe through a riffle. After two slight bends, we pass under the tall Hwy 2 bridge. The banks past the bridge are thick with Willow bushes and Loosestrife and topped by scrubby Oak and Manitoba Maple. The water is deeper and we can't see bottom. Orange Jewelweed blossoms glow like coals in the shade of grapevined Manitoba Maples, and Wild Cucumber makes curved crests of frothy white flower spikes along horizontal boughs.

The banks have become taller with more pine and Ash, and we see a section of sandy bluff ahead. An Osprey takes off from a high snag. I note a Cicada's whine, and then a helicopter's stuttering thunder overhead. A big dragonfly cruises past us, faster than we paddle. A dainty Solitary Sandpiper steps quickly through the shallows, peeping and teetering, its breast reflecting the warm tones of a sandbar.

The mouth of the Rouge, looking east

Boys fishing from the west bank shout to us that they've caught a 40 cm Salmon on a spinning lure today. The low wet willow land to the east rises into a wooded slope. We slip past an opening in the trees, and there, down a high, short-grassed bank runs a flight of wooden steps, like a ladder let down from the house at the top.

We examine tracks on the narrow muddy beach of the west shore. The soft wet surface is printed by Deer hooves and Raccoon hands, and littered with the brown curls of fallen Manitoba Maple leaves. A dense green jungle of Ostrich Ferns fills the space beneath the Maples. Grapevines climb the trunks and drape horizontal branches with heavy sleeves of green above the river bank. The hand-sized Grape leaves above our heads sparkle with insect pinholes, and beneath them, at arm's length, hang bunches of opalescent baby Grapes.

A little downstream Fred spots a Painted Turtle perched on the highest stub of a barkless branch protruding from the water. Its dusty dry shell shows that it has been basking for some time. As we slip beyond its branch, the turtle is scared into the water by another party of canoeists who, talking and splashing, hadn't noticed it. Another Solitary Sandpiper is walking daintily along a log. A Great Blue Heron, its back very blue in the sun, flies up from its fishing spot and heads upstream on broad wings, croaking in a perturbed way, "Always People in canoes ruining my fishing."

The east bank becomes bluff-like here, and we're coming into the open space of the Rouge Marsh, with a low grape-draped hedge of Purple Loosestrife on the west, and beyond it the waving tops of the Cattail marsh. Then a long bank of Loosestrife and Goldenrod screens the open space of a lagoon to the east whose far shore rises up in a high treed bank with houses atop.

Zigzagging downstream, our channel meanders into open marsh in a broad curve to the west. Coming east again, we see the railway bridge and the footbridge, a clear tube with a grey framework. The banks and bridges frame a view of open sky space over Lake Ontario, with only a sand beach bar separating the river and the sky. To make a brief exploration of the marsh, we turn west into a stiff wind, close under outward-leaning purple and green plants of Loosestrife, to the open water of the lagoon. The south shore is bounded by a road and

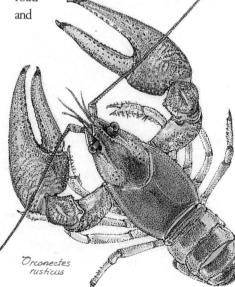

Orconectes rusticus

95

parking lot, with a steep green railway embankment above. Soon our senses are filled by the rush and whistle of an 18-car GO train.

A few Blue-winged Teal fly across a marshscape distinguished by the prominent white shapes of several Mute Swans. On a bird-tracked mudbar, a large swan stands to preen itself with tangerine-orange bill behind a big patch of swan-white waterlilies. *Nymphaea odorata*, which stand tiptoe in the water like pointed petally ballerinas, their yellow centres faintly orange-scented. A Honey Bee lands to drink water drops from a lily pad. Two Killdeer are bathing at the edge of a mudflat where a peep Sandpiper forages, stepping and pecking. A brown-winged Osprey courses overhead as we paddle back to the parking lot. The water temperature is 25°C in the main channel of the river. The shore is crowded with People, some fishing and some feeding bread to birds, and the lagoon is crowded with Mute Swans, Geese, Mallards and Great Blue Herons. One Great Egret stands white and tall among the other birds.

The canoe is beached on the riverbank, and Fred and Lee Ann depart by car to retrieve the truck, and

leave her to trek back to us from Frenchman's Bay. Jennie makes friends on the sandy beach, tumbling an air mattress in the small breaking waves, as I shelter from the wind and the mid-afternoon sun, just behind the corner of the Canoe Club building, to draw. First I squint west toward the bluff-like end of Rouge Hill, a narrow ridge truncated by the lake, and draw it in ink, silhouetted against the brilliance of sand, lake and sky.

Fred returns with the truck just as I begin the watercolour wash for the sky, looking east toward the Pickering Nuclear Plant bathed in the rosy glow of late sunshine. He sits against the wall beside me and notes birds: passing flocks of Cormorants and Canada Geese over the lake, Mallards in the river, a few Great Blackback and Herring Gulls on the river mouth bar and 150 Ringbills there and on the beach, Common Terns fishing over the lake, and an Osprey, soaring over on stiff wings. Gulls don't believe that Ospreys only eat fish, and they get up in a big flock as it goes over. A few Pigeons forage out from the steel beams of the railway trestle.

Frenchman's Bay, Pickering, 27 August
A cloudy evening. Jennie plays ball with a local family on the goose-clipped lawn of Bruce Hanscombe Park. I stand at the grassy edge of a steep shaly bank to do this ink drawing of sleeping sailboats, the long thin wooded sandbar with a small gap to Lake Ontario, a red navigation light and the bulky cylindrical reactors of the nuclear power plant at Pickering. A Great Blackback Gull loafs on a buoy. A few motor launches loiter along the bay side of the bar, but retire to their berths in the marina at the southeast corner of the bay before I've finished my drawing.

In the map Fred sketches in his journal, the habitats all around the bay are noted: East of the wooded sandbar the Pickering nuclear plant looms and north of the plant bristles a densely packed marina of mixed boats. The shore curves north-northwest in tall beds of Cattails that front residential woodlands, to a large low apartment-like building of grey concrete at the northeast corner. Sharp-edged stands of hybrid Cattails rim the north end of the bay, and to the northwest the Community Centre, which was our Frenchmans Bay auditory station, is screened by stands of Willows.

South of the Cattails, Hanscombe Park bulges into the bay, an armoured lawn-park with masses of geese and huge, drooping Black Willows. Cattails and a Trumpeter Swan occupy a storm sewer delta. Shrubs of narrow-leaved Willows and past-flower Purple Loosestrife line the western shore below where I stand to draw, and continue south toward the yacht club docks. Just south of the moored boats stretches a long thin line of green-grown sandbar with telephone wires. Three adult Blackcrown Nightherons fly past, deploying to night stations around the still bay under a quiet grey stratus overcast.

Lee Ann wrote from the mouth of the bay, where she walked the sandy promenade along the lake, about a Spotted Sandpiper that ran past her along the water's edge on delicate legs, and about the slope of green lawn that runs up to a children's play structure, as she looked north along the west shore. Farther back in the distance, beyond the marshes at the head of the bay, rushes the 401 highway, and before it, on an embankment embroidered with the vines of Black Swallowwort, the green and white snake of a GO train slithers by on its treetop course.

Night lights begin to blink on in the suburbs, and in the tall apartment

97

building northeast of the bay. The last speedboat rushes by, someone's party music following close in its wake, and a few straggling yachts return to their nests in the mast forest. A sign on the beach claims that water here is unsafe for bathing. The bright lights and bubble tops of the nuclear reactors glow against the darkening sky, as indigo night extinguishes the last few strands of pinkish cloud.

Listening from our Frenchmans Bay auditory station at the edge of the marsh below the Community Centre parking lot, we have never heard anything but Toads and Canada Geese.

Duffins Creek at Saylor Road, Ajax, 26 August

We came to this silty creek in its willow-dominated floodplain looking for the crayfish *Orconectes rusticus*. Tall yellow Jerusalem Artichokes are in bloom in a patch in alluvial mud just downstream of the bridge, and the streamside mud is patterned with many Raccoon tracks. Hundreds of Ringbill Gulls sail slowly overhead.

Lifting small rocks just downstream of the bridge, in shallow water, we uncover many juvenile *Orconectes propinquus* and a few *O. virilis*. The rest of the creek bottom as far up or down as we can see is just silt or silty drifts of sand. A few *O. rusticus*, which we found in the Rouge River, were discovered in the upper reaches of Duffins Creek in 1983 and 1985, but they have evidently not spread downstream this far. These crayfish, native to the Ohio Valley, established populations in Wisconsin,

Minnesota, northern Ontario, New York and Maine, where they were released as fish bait. In Lake of the Woods, we found them replacing the native *O. virilis* at the rate of nearly a metre a day over the course of 10 years, but in southern Ontario they don't seem quite as intrusive or damaging.

We return to Lynde Shores Camp after a downpour of rain.

Duffins Creek to Lynde Shores, Ajax & Whitby, 25 August

Turbid green water is being driven upstream from the lake now, while a 100 Geese and 50 Ringbill Gulls loaf on a bar in channel. Drab green cattail marsh extends uniformly from the far creek-bank to the little bluff below the fields of Squires Beach. Ten Common Terns are fishing and calling.

We came here to leave Fred and Jennie at the Duffins Creek Rotary Park to walk back to Lynde Shores. Before I leave, Fred walks out to the tip of the east beach bar, across from the shore where we found the shell-rich drift this spring. A juvenile Bonaparte's Gull rests there, the first we have seen this season (and the only one we were to see). The sand and gravel bar at the mouth of the creek has been trampled by People, who evidently placed the traffic direction sign in the middle of the channel mouth. Under Poplars on the brushy bar Fred found a thicket of Dull-leaf Indigobush and a plant of white-flowered Comfrey, but there are no Painted Turtles basking where he saw them in May.

A lawn-park runs all along the eastern Ajax waterfront, and Fred and Jennie walked east to Lions Point (Simcoe Point on the topo map) along the asphalt-paved bikeway to a plastic-planked park bench. The rocks at the edge of the shore are felted with green algae. On the 20-m bluff face of massive silt, only a few scattered herbs grow – Carrot, Goldenrod, Yarrow, Yellow Sweet Clover and Evening Primrose – but Apple and Hawthorn bushes poke out and up from just below the lip of the bluff.

INY Chironomid gnats danced in a cloud around them as they walked, and a swarm of "Black Snow" Caddisflies lilted back and forth above the bike pathway. A field to the north is left to naturalize with tall grasses and wildflowers. It is randomly spotted with nursery trees: Ash, Spruce, Mountain Ash, Aspen, pendulous Birch and Cottonwood. Farther north are mowed fields and beyond them the lakeshore road and neighbourhoods of close-packed houses.

As Fred and Jennie continued along the trail, six boldly striped migrant Savannah Sparrows glanced up at them from the beach and flew away. Then the bluffs are notched down to a height of only 3 m, where a storm sewer flows brook-clear into the lake, probably following the route of an aboriginal stream. They climbed down beside the outfall and rested on boulders. On the dry bluff face, Black Swallowwort was wilting in the heat, and the thermometer read 29°C. A slurry of algal fibres slurped among the rocks, washing the head and skin of a dead Sucker.

They followed the beach below the lawn-park, at the foot of 8-m bluffs which replayed the cliffs of Scarborough in miniature with slides, slumps, chunks of black shale and silty blocks. They crossed masses of algal felt, dead on the upper beach and green and live on the lower, with plastic objects tangled all through it: tennis balls, fishing floats, a Barbie Doll's bra, a rubber snake and a McDonalds Earth Day blue plastic tray. Jennie found one crayfish cheliped.

They stopped at the tip of a rounded point to have a bite of supper and look east towards camp. Sitting on a bluff-foot boulder at the water's edge, and shaded by small Willows, Silver Maples, Ashes and Poplars, Jennie drew a Caspian Tern fishing from the clear sky.

They scrambled back up to the conveniently level path. Then, looking down, Fred thought he saw some good drift below, and encouraged Jennie to slide down the 7-m face of the bluff to the beach again. The bluff was not as smooth as they'd expected, and the descent ripped her pants and reddened her backside, so Fred hurried down to console her, and found the line of drift to be barren of invertebrates. The beach was deep beds of flattish gravel, with the wrecked steel lining and rebar of storm sewer culverts protruding from the bluff like the exposed entrails of some anatomically complicated beast. A little east, Jennie bathed her slide abrasions in the chlorinated outflow from the Durham Region Water Treatment Plant. This broad channel, crossed by a wooden bridge and dammed by a gravel bar, proved barren of animals, as are so many streams associated with water plants.

Toward the east end of the curiously-named Ajax By-Law Park, the bluffs rise in height, and are increasingly armoured by old sections of concrete culverts. Black Swallowwort was prominent along the bluff brink, and they sampled the bright red fruit of an Apple tree. Descending into a residential area, they passed another, much more relaxed, park where the lawns were shaded by big Silver Maples, Willows and Ashes, and ditches lush with Cattails. The water was clear on the beach but signs warned that it was unsafe for swimming or bathing.

West of the mouth of Carruthers Creek, a signed barrier warned of a biting Dog on private property, so they detoured inland along the road to our Pickering Beach auditory station at a bridge over Carruthers Creek between a housing subdivision, old fields and lakeshore marsh. They left the road to follow a path that parallels the creek through a narrow Hawthorn, Apple, Cherry and Beech woods. The forest floor herbs were all wilted with drought. The path ended at a big multitrunked Red Oak, much used for climbing and nailed about with tree forts.

At the mudflats of the Carruthers Creek marsh, Raccoon tracks marked the mud of the Cattail shore, and ducks, Geese, Yellowlegs and many other shorebirds were feeding and loafing in the open water of the marsh. It was too muddy to move along the shore of the marsh, so they crossed an old field toward a hedgerow of Hawthorn, disturbing a flock of roosting Great Blue Herons. When they reached Richardson Point along the hedgerow, the lake was pale with sunset light.

At the foot of 10-m gravel bluffs, they walked along the flat roadlike surface of sediment washed down from the cliffs. In the fading light this beach seemed a sort of charnel house, littered with dead and dying Herring Gulls, a large dead *Oncorhynchus* salmon, many dead Carp, and the bones and teeth of Cattle.

Then Fred and Jennie hurried past houses that reach their artifacts down the bluff to the narrow beach: concrete or metal stairways, seawalls, breakwaters made of tires and boats on little crank-up racks. When they stopped to measure two Toads caught by headlamp at the water's edge they saw my light-flash signal from camp. Along the Cranberry Marsh beach bar they found a Green Frog and a Leopard Frog on the beach and east of Cranberry Marsh they began to see more Toads.

Lynde Shores to Port Whitby, Whitby, 28 August
We were up at 05:30 this morning to leave for home, to check on the house and gardens, and to bring our big Dog Bear back with us. Lee Ann was awake before we left, in a few scatters of rain, feeling somewhat sad that her summer was ending with her return to university tomorrow. The wind forced up huge muddy black-grey waves, and Cormorants flew by as she ate her breakfast of rice porridge on the beach.

Inspired by wind and waves she set off at 07:13 to walk toward the surf that she saw breaking on the armoured shores at Port Whitby.

ILLOWS, Manitoba Maples and Cottonwoods all showed the undersides of their leaves, and Cormorants struggled past in the southwest wind. A slim, cautious Great Blue Heron strode away as she approached the mouth of Lynde Creek, where six juvenile and two adult Great Blackback Gulls stood with their beaks into the wind, and Ringbill Gulls were on the beach or in the air, flapping yet hardly moving.

She soaked her feet crossing the deep creek channel, swollen by the rush and escape of lake water. A single swan floated serenely on Storey Marsh, which winds back to Victoria Street like a wide river, edged by thick fields of tall straight Cattails. Its inner curves are wooded with Willow, Paper Birch, and some already-flame-topped Red Maples. Orange-pink light from the early morning sun caught the frothy waves of the lake, but at close hand Lee Ann could see they were full of sand, green algae and black bits of stick and bark.

She followed a Willow-arboured path up from the beach and crossed a dry 10-m wide outflow ditch bedded with crumbled rocks and covered with large-gauge chicken wire. Green-or-ange-stained muck retreated between the rocks and rimmed the few pools of standing water. Huge blocks of black-ened concrete barricaded the ditch and the shoreline, where the breaking spray was highest.

The path opened up into mowed lawn and a road beside six old water sedimentation beds, about half a metre deep, their bottoms cracked and dry with varicoloured sediment. A huge ramp into the lake, something like a boat launch, had presumably been the outflow of this sewage treatment plant. Behind a screen of Willows is the Sun-day-silent construction site of the new wing of the Whitby Psychiatric Hospi-tal, and big new houses with cherry red and forest green roofs and gables.

Lee Ann crossed the lawn of the hospital, treed with Silver Maple, Wil-lows, a *Magnolia* and numerous Scots Pine, all dampened by spray from the surf 20 m below. Rounding the east side of the point, she found a beach of rocks and boulders, swishing their green "mermaid hair" in the agitated lake. For a while she walked above a gravel beach, and then the shore be-came armoured. Noticing a lower path that parallelled the top of the armoured seawall, she cut down from the lawn to walk where it wound pleasantly through dry grass, flowering Goldenrod and Al-ders. Strolling beneath Manitoba Ma-ples and Pines, to the accompaniment of cricket and grasshopper song, she came eventually to a deeply rutted laneway and Iroquois Beach.

This was a sandy beach littered with broken bottles, cigarette butts, plastic straws and charred remains of beach fires. Trash barrels hid among young Poplars under mature Basswood and Willows. A couple out with their coffee and Dogs were as surprised as Lee Ann to see someone else out so early on

Sunday. The wind filled her ears, and a hollow percussion of rolling, clattering stones filled the roar of the waves.

Half a kilometre east, she arrived at the outer point of Port Whitby. Standing on the pier of the yacht club, she was showered by the lake as it hammered against the corrugated steel breakwater. Even inside, against the stone pier of the nearest marina, the waves kept crashing, as if to tear away all barriers. Wind whistled through the forest of masts, singing in the rigging. Boats rocked back and forth and their cables hummed like cello strings and clanked like chimes.

Returning to camp, she was glad she hadn't come later, as the stormy lake had cut the mouth of Lynde Creek wider and deeper. Waves and creek water in turn were surging ominously through the gap, though it proved only knee-deep. A Great Blue Heron with a big fish in its beak stilt-walked away from her, then slowly flew to a low branch as she crashed through the water.

She came past a nearly adult Herring Gull hunched up on the uppermost drift line of the beach. We saw it again when Fred, Jennie and I returned to camp, and it was dead on the morning of 2 September. Three days later Fred turned the carcase over and saw an aluminum band on one leg. It was very emaciated and had been moulting its primary feathers. We telephoned its number, 1016-56896, to the CWS in Ottawa, and the report from the banding office indicates that it was banded as a nestling on 10 June 1993, near Barbeau, south of Sault Ste. Marie, Michigan.

Whitby waterfront, 1 September
At 16:07 Fred bicycled from our camp at Lynde Shores, east along Victoria Street. Past the Whitby Psychiatric Hospital he turned down Brock Street at Thickson Road and coasted down a gentle slope to Port Whitby, where he stopped at the mud-and-Cattail inlet to the harbour. Here he found a close-cropped lawn park thronged with Geese and surrounded by the fields and lots of an industrial neighbourhood. A garbage basket was stuffed with plastic bags from bread fed to birds, and the site appeared little changed from our visit in April. Geese still wandered carelessly across the road, paying scant heed to the honking horns of the cars that always stop for them.

He cycled past boatyards, railway tracks, industrial old fields and woods to the west shore of the mouth of Whitby Harbour, where he picked the Flowering Rush that I have drawn. This lovely and robust rush grows along a little ditch in a lawn-park between a water filtration plant and the long breakwater piers that guard the harbour.

In terms of the circulation of the lake, this is the halfway point in our journey. Along the shore we have passed, the net movement of sediment has been westward, toward deposition on the Toronto Islands and Hamilton Beach, or in the embayments of the new lake-fill parks. East of here sediment will be moving with us, towards deposition on the beaches of Presqu'ile. This eastward movement is driven by the prevailing southwesterlies, while westward movement is driven by the greater fetch and strength of storm winds from the northeast.

Flowering Rush

Eastward, the bluffs rise to the end of South Blair Road, marked by a line of Slippery Elms. At the brink of the 12-m bluff, Fred sat above the cross-wrinkled blue lake, jumbled concrete slabs and slumped soil springing up with Coltsfoot. A plume of smoke from a high stack on the horizon was the first sign we have seen of New York State. He followed a sketchy little path beyond the fence into flat land between the bluff edge and the fenceline of a steel mill, because this was the planned route of the Waterfront Trail. He pushed his bike through fields of Goldenrod and Dogwood, where migrating Monarchs sailed with a juvenile Harrier, both rich orange, and both rocking in flight. Then he lost the trail in a field of Rapeseed stubble.

At 18:00 he saw Monarchs gathering for the evening, their parallel orange wings serrating tall stalks of Horseweed and making one branch of an Ash tree look like a late autumn Oak. After pushing through 600 m of trackless Goldenrod, he reached a deep ditch with a fast dark flow at the bottom. It took half an hour to find the best place to descend, and he scrambled up the other side, dragging his bike behind him. He came out in a herbicidally-weeded Corn field, where in places Field Horsetail formed an undercrop of delicate green. He couldn't push the bike through the Corn crop to Thicksons Point, so he wheeled north along its edge toward the steel mill, where a migrating Sharp-shinned Hawk was hunting over tumuli of waste with quick short downstrokes. Skirting the outlying structures of the mill, he passed through an industrial park onto Wentworth Street. After attempts to find the prospective trail on Thickson Point and the Corbett Creek Sewage Treatment Plant, he cycled along to Philip Murray Avenue in Oshawa to wait for me to trace the road part of his mapped route and pick him up. He spent two hours waiting at the entrance to brightly-lit baseball and tennis fields. Venus set gleaming in the west over a pale yellow-brown sunset, unseen Killdeer called, and People played tennis and baseball far into the night.

At length he decided I was not coming and headed back to camp. I returned at dawn, from where I'd waited at our planned rendezvous, having expected Fred to push on to McLaughlin Bay, and not thinking of retracing the trail route until too late.

Lynde Shores Beach, Whitby, 3 September

In the evening we walk Bear down to the western beach. The lake, just before dark, is disappearing, a calm reflection of the paling sky, water as light as air, pearl grey-pink and grey-blue, and I feel as if the lake and the sky are two halves of a pale-nacred clam, encasing us in a world of mother-of-pearl. We walk past the old Cottonwood that lies out across the beach, and further, to the solemn swooshing of little waves tripping on the fine gravel beach, and the music of Canada Geese gathering offshore, barely discernible on the water.

Then we see the young Great Black-back Gull, big and perfect, lying against the sand, its nobility scarcely diminished by death. Tail end and wing tips are black, and its back is tweedy with half-black. The black bill is blunt, curved and powerful. We talk about the fierce, predatory habits of its kind and call it, respectfully, "Sea Raven." Fred walks back with Bear, and I draw it lying on the leaf-sprinkled sand, through the last of the evening light. As I lift it, the wings spread nearly as far as I can stretch my arms. Its body is surprisingly light to carry back to camp. We found areas of hemorrhage on the neck and one wing, and it was not emaciated, so we suppose it was shot.

Oshawa waterfront, 5 September

Leaving Jennie and me to explore Darlington Park from McLaughlin Bay, Fred continued east from Oshawa's Lakeshore West Park, where he had waited for me after dark on 1 September. Killdeer called as he crossed the lawns and followed a mown path across fields of Goldenrod to Gold Point. A little stream runs out there to the beach, under spreading Willow trees beyond a bit of Cattail marsh. The same windless surf was breaking here as rolled in all day in camp. A Spotted Sandpiper and a Kingfisher flew up from the beach and a flock of Cormorants, mostly juveniles, was periscoping over the chop offshore. The short coarse gravel bar at the mouth did not close the creek, and the waves pushed a green slurry of algal fibres up into the shallow creek.

The Gold Point stream originates north of Philip Murray Drive; it comes down to the road in a concrete culvert from a stormwater retention pond bounded by two dams of stone-filled gabions. This is evidently the runoff from the vast multi-vented General Motors plant to the north, ponded for gradual release, as a sign near water controls admonished, "Do not let the creek go dry." A few Geese

wing chord 466 cm.

and Mallards rested on the muddy pondshore.

He biked south down Stephenson Road between old fields and a subdivision and then paralleled the shore, ducking through looping streets lined with young trees, and turning down a lane to a brick-paved play area, swarming with children and mothers. Below them a wide lake-edge flat ran out to the water; Goldenrod dominated the fields, with scattered Hawthorn bushes and patches of cattails.

West of the Murac subdivision at Park Road the lakeside commons disappeared. House lots ran down to the lake, with older brick houses and more mature trees. At the end of the road a sign forbids use of the steep path of packed silt down the 15-m bluff to the storm sewer outfall and the wave-washed gravel beach.

He continued along lakeside streets to a paved asphalt bike path along the north side of Pumphouse Marsh. From the lookout tower he saw two Mute Swans on the shallow duckweed-covered pond, lined with Cattails along the north shore, beds of Iris and Arrowhead along the west side, and on the southeast, *Decodon.* When we visited the marsh in the spring, we followed a little footpath that runs along lake dunes on the south side. Fred watched 10 Nighthawks catching insects overhead. Dipping and wheeling, their wing-patches flashed in the sunset.

The new asphalt trail took him past the water filtration plant and lawn-parks to a high headland. From this vantage point he looked east in a pre-view of the next eight days of exploration; across a beach-fronted lawn-park, the mouth of Oshawa Harbour, the woods of the Second Marsh reserve and the General Motors headquarters above McLaughlin Bay, Darlington Park and field-topped bluffs beyond, to the St. Marys Cement Plant in Port Darlington.

Packing up his notes, he whizzed down to the lawn-park with its picnic tables, big Maples and play structures. There he walked his bicycle out onto what at first appeared to be a natural sand beach. Soon he realized sand had been hauled here and spread inland of a coarse gravel beach covered with algal felt. A long pier reached from the mouth of Oshawa Creek to the fresh air of the lake. Its white railings were lined with fishermen whipping the lake and creek with long flexible spinning rods and minnow-like lures.

The trail turns inland to cross Oshawa Creek on Simcoe Street. There Fred watched the clear greenish lakewater slowly flowing upstream between low banks of tallgrass industrial land. The trails that follow Oshawa Creek north must branch off somewhere here, but he didn't see any sign of them as he bicycled on past a relatively inactive industrial area, old fields and oil tank farms, and a branch of the creek still and green above a marina.

He hurried past a few small houses, alfalfa fields, some businesses – "39 acres industrial for sale" – and old fields of Goldenrod with Manitoba Maple on the lot lines. Then he pedalled up the slope of Colonel Sam

Drive, past the sewage treatment
plant with its perpetual flame,
and along the road past Harmony
Creek and the grassy paths at the
north end of the Second Marsh
reserve.

A wide expanse of old fields yellow
in Goldenrod slope down from Colonel Sam Drive, and one Nighthawk
dipped and twisted over it. Venus
shone jewel-like in the pale sunset
reflecting on the water of Second Marsh, which was dot-
ted with clots of geese.
The asphalt road that
leads to the General Motors offices is
lined with sapling Ash and Norway
Maple and the streetlights were just
coming on as sunset settled to peach
red on the northwest horizon, and the
Nighthawk was replaced by a large bat.

He remembered his visit to the
mouth of Second Marsh on his trip
home on 31 July, finding wide areas of
waterlilies with large fish jumping, Cedar Waxwing flocks in the Cottonwoods, and Swans, Geese and herons
on the outer bars of McLaughlin Bay.
Inland from the beach, dense stands of
white Sweet Clover were attended only
by Bumblebees and Syrphid flies, and
he wondered if the absence of Honey
Bees was due to environmental pollution, Tracheal Mites or both.

As he waited for Jennie and me by
the truck in the parking lot of the Second Marsh Trail, Venus became
brighter, joined by Jupiter to south and
then by Mars overhead, and stars. Then

Joe Pye Weed
Eupatorium
maculatum

he bicycled east into Darlington Park
to find us.

**Darlington Park, Clarington,
5 September**
Jennie, Bear and I take the footpath
into Darlington Provincial Park from
the road on the west side of
McLaughlin Bay. The Willow woods
have a misty-green carpet of Jewelweed,
low and level like duckweed on a pond.
It grows taller, sparked with orange
blossoms in sunny patches. Then the
Willows give way to a canopy of Silver
Maple's sharply cut leaves. Suddenly we
arrive at a smooth paved road that
leads us south past a tallgrass field full
of Poplars, Cottonwoods and Willows.
Full bushy Hawthorn trees with ser-
rated leaves are fruited with small ap-
ple-like haws.

From the lawn and parking lot, the
shore of McLaughlin Bay is lined with
concrete slabs. A dock stretches out
into the bay, and fishermen in a boat

106

are reflected in the mirror-smooth water as they cast, first on one side and then on the other. Beyond them the lake glances over a long thin bar which is joined from the east by a series of Willow-covered dunes and bars and a short line of Cottonwoods.

Leaving our supper picnic table, we follow a pleasant mowed path through meadow parkland. Our way is flanked by long grasses, and fruiting trees and bushes: tall Mountain Ashes hung with bright scarlet bunches, thickly leaved Crabapples with small green fruits, and cascades of the ever-present Grapevine. The trail follows a curved, willow-lined shore to the base of the sandy bar across McLaughlin Bay, affording a view to the east of low sandy bluffs with wooded parkland atop. We walk past picnic tables on the beach, and return to the path, past venerable Black Willows, giant and many-trunked, to a picnic lawn atop a hill. We pick up the trail again at the park's restored Pioneer Log Cabin and follow it away from the lake, collecting a flower head of Joe Pye Weed to paint from a tall clump growing with great golden banners of 2 m high Goldenrod.

The trail splits and we choose the path that continues along the lake, but it brings us soon to the mouth of Robinson Creek. We follow this stony bottomed brook for a little way beneath tall Willows, cross it by an arched wooden footbridge, and enter the campground past a small brick office. Threading our way through the thickly wooded campground, noting an impressive mixture of native tree species,

we reach the shore again at a chainlink fence along the top of steep bluffs. At the eastern end of the fence we sit at the brink to enjoy a sunset view of the turquoise and salmon lake lapping its curved sandy shore. A Cherry tree juts horizontally from mid-bluff below us. Gentle swells swirl around a line of boulders just offshore, covering and uncovering, and an algae-stained rocky beach stretches to the east.

Two water-skidoos buzz past like crazed Bumblebees, dipping and bucking and sending up fountains of spray on each side. After they're gone, a close troop of six Blackcrown Nightherons wing along the shore, and a flock of gulls streams close to the water, heading for wherever they spend the night.

Hurrying east past the last campsites in the falling dusk, we meet a dark wall of evergreen boughs, a close plantation of Spruce. To see what lies east of the boundary of Darlington Park we press past Dogwood bushes and Goldenrod on an exceedingly narrow path along the brink of the bluff, finding the trail broken in a couple of places by grooves eroded down the cliff. After about 100 m of this beautiful but hazardous course we come suddenly to a narrow gully and the end of the Spruce plantation. A flat field of Soybean plants, tall and green, stretches out ahead of us, totally unlike anything we've seen all day.

We re-cross the top of the gully and step carefully back along the bluff to the campground. Hurrying north, past campsites occupied by tree-shadowed dusk, and empty lawns and lighted

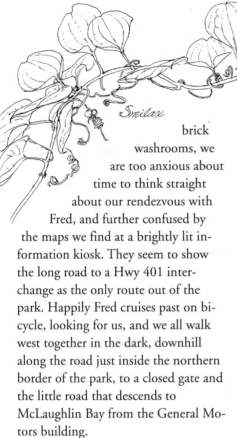

Smilax

brick washrooms, we are too anxious about time to think straight about our rendezvous with Fred, and further confused by the maps we find at a brightly lit information kiosk. They seem to show the long road to a Hwy 401 interchange as the only route out of the park. Happily Fred cruises past on bicycle, looking for us, and we all walk west together in the dark, downhill along the road just inside the northern border of the park, to a closed gate and the little road that descends to McLaughlin Bay from the General Motors building.

Lynde Creek, Whitby, 7 September
Before driving east, we pay a visit to Lynde Creek, after having crossed it back and forth countless times during our camp at Lynde Shores. Now, on our last day here we trundle our trailer through the gate and park it in the Conservation Authority's recreation area picnic lot.

Back through the gate, we walk across the little bridge over the arm of the marsh that receives the western inlet stream, and wander up two of the paths that lead into the woods from the

road to see the *Smilax* vines that Fred has found. The first has big oval leaves and drapes in a heavy bower from trees to the bank. A little farther along and on the east side of the road, the one I have drawn here with smaller, rounder leaves, crawls up into a thicket of Blackberry and Goldenrod. South of Ontario most Smilaxes are woody and thorny. Catbriar makes impenetrable thorny tangles in the southern woods, but our species, *Smilax herbacea*, Carrionflower, is thornless and herbaceous, dying back each year to grow again from the roots.

I sit, sketching, at the base of a big Black Willow near the bridge. It lowers its limbs to the water for ducks to stand on. The duck-dabbling peace is broken now and again by flurries of chasing and water-thrashing, just like children in a swimming pool. I count more than 50 Mallards.

The water is greyish with stirred sediment. The ducks crowd and churn to reach bread crusts that children toss in. Out beyond the willow shade, floating duckweed covers the surface like thick green paint. Water Lily leaves mark its sunny serenity with folds and ruffles. Ducks plough through the placid green water-field, dabbling with snippy little bill movements, leaving short paths of dark open water which soon close again behind them. The wind is autumn-fresh, and the duck-weed smells like lettuce.

A Painted Turtle basks like a lily pond ornament, unperturbed by a duck preening vigorously just centimetres away. A wind-lifted lily pad raises and lowers, sun motes twinkle, windy willow leaves wave and rush, spray explodes from bathing ducks, and all through this motion the turtle keeps basking.

Now I hear a volley of hoarse peeps, tossed back and forth among a family of five Gallinules (Common Moorhens) over by the wall of waving Cattails. I focus the spotting scope on a group of four adults and four juveniles as they lift their long thin toes out of the water in front of them and pull water lily leaves underwater to stand on. They are quieter than the ducks. Up to their breasts in water but stepping as they move, they peck at water plants, a bit of lily leaf and some pondweed and an insect or two. The adults are blue-black in front, with bright orange bills. The young have dark bills and brown and grey plumage, marked white on each side of the tail like the glint on the edge of an upturned lily leaf. Through the

magical lenses of my scope, I've forgotten time and abandoned myself contentedly to life as a Gallinule. Only with great reluctance will I return to my "human responsibilities."

Fred walked out to the end of the Lynde Shores Marsh Boardwalk which slices through a dense stand of Cattail. A stiff wind blows from the northwest. Scarlet-bodied Dragonflies, mating, land to rest on the boardwalk in the shelter of the cattails. In the open water of the marsh float large rafts of the leaves of White Waterlily.

Jennie has found the children of another home-schooling family and is walking with them, feeding ducks, Chipmunks and black and grey Squirrels, and persuading Chickadees to land on their hands, but now she must say goodbye, for it's time to move to our next camp.

10

Port Darlington Camp

West Beach, Port Darlington, Clarington, 13 September

We have our own bit of beach at this camp, with the trailer backed snugly between a Cedar hedge and a boarded-up cottage. The rear window looks out over yellow autumn grasses, and clean buffy-tan sand with a row of pebbles, to the lake.

There is a richness in the way the mood of the lake changes from day to day and hour to hour. I did the painting of St. Marys Cement pier on 8 September under a threatening sky, just to record purple storm colour on clear water green. Since then we have enjoyed a couple of days of land breeze that slicked the swells flat so that Jennie could swim in

clear water as calm as a pond.

Where the West Beach Road turns to run along the beach it is lined on the lake side with houses and cottages, some old, some renovated or new, and mostly well kept. Past a pair of concrete blocks the neighbourhood changes, being mostly owned by the Harbour Company and leased to tenants, many of whom have been residents there for much of their lives. A lady who was walking across the sandy alley to a neighbour's told me she and her husband first met in the old Dance Hall which now is just a long black roof lying on rubble, and the old store is gone too. The houses at the end of the road are three and four deep along sandy alleys and some are

empty,
but not all. As I draw
cottages among snow-like drifts of
sand, black field crickets are carrying
on flirtations, courtships and territorial
disputes in the dry yellow grass by a
pile of wooden planks beside me.

Darlington Park to Port Darlington, Clarington, 8 September

Fred intends to take a bike trip today
so we've been watching eerily complex
changes and turnings of wind, rain and
surf, as if the weather's been casting
back and forth, mandated to rain on
the just but not the unjust. Fred's not
sure which we are.

He took a short walk along the
beach from our Port Darlington camp,
finding some snail shells and dead balloons in the drift line, pink-dyed
salmon eggs in a net bag, a green and
red golf tee and one Alewife. A
Sanderling foraged too,
pecking invisible parti-
cles along the edges of
the tumbling sandy
waves. Fred discovered
a few plants of Sea
Rocket, *Cakile edentula*, in

bloom and
picked some leaves for his sand-
wiches.

In the afternoon we trucked Fred
and his bicycle, equipped with rain
gear, back to Darlington Park, to work
eastward to camp. He found a road-
killed Garter Snake where the park
road crosses Robinson Creek, and
then slid down an embankment past
Jewelweed and *Bidens*, to where the
muddy creek flows under tall Willow
trees.

He found *Physa* snails on a stony
bottom, and a muddy bottom dotted
with European Ear Snails. There were a
few minnows but no crayfish or frogs,
and the surface twinkled with the footprints of big *Gerris* water striders.

Leaving the second-growth mixed
woods of the park, he cycled past a
field of Pumpkins and another of

They come up to the
surface to breathe,
and swing their shells
violently through 90°
when touched by
a neighbour.

European
Ear Snails
*Radix
auricularia*

1.5 m. tall, with the finest velvet all over its leaves and stem.

yellow flowered Velvet Leaf, Abutilon theophrasti from India

curious steers, and then turned south on Courtice Road to explore the gravel-bar mouth of Tooley Creek, finding one crayfish claw and a view of bluffs to the east and west along the lake. I met him by a field of Soybeans along the 401 service road, and we picked a plant of the tall weed Velvetleaf, naturalized from India, for me to draw.

Cycling past fields of Corn, Alfalfa and Oats, Fred soon came to the long stretch of chainlink and barbed-wire fencing that encloses the brushy fields and second-growth forests of the nuclear plant and St. Marys Cement Company. At the Darlington Nuclear Plant's public entrance, he was greeted by another striking yellow flowered composite, Cup Plant, with leaves joined in cups about its strong flat-sided stems, growing in weedy vigour among underfertilized nursery plantings.

Port Darlington to Wilmot Creek, Clarington, 10 September

This afternoon Fred began his walk east along the CN tracks, from an industrial park by Hwy 401. At first, the landscape was dominated by electric wires. Fencing strands surround the pastures. A sparse array of single wire CN telegraph wires run between cross-trees of weathered poles along the tracks, and newer cabled wires run directly between the poles. The hydro lines that feed electricity to the few houses are protected by a scaffolding of tall poles where they run under the high-tension lines strung on huge pagoda-profile towers that march eastward from the Darlington Nuclear Plant. These sound like a conversational flock of metallic waterbirds, presumably because the swaying wires turn the wheel-like structures they are suspended from.

On the grassy embankment at the limestone railway bridge there was a sparse stand of dark green *Lithospermum officinale*, which we call the Perth-

Weigh-Station-Pearlseed, having first marvelled at its tiny teardrop seedcases at a stop along Hwy 7. Walking along through pastures and old fields, he met a Woodchuck which dashed to the cover of a grassy railway embankment. He passed through a deep cutting where a grassy slope supports a little grove of Elms and Ashes. Past a gravel road railway crossing, he cut eastward to Wilmot Drive. The blooms of Goldenrods were beginning to open, a patch of Fireweed was in fluffy fruit beside a trailer storage lot, and Elderberries were ripening.

The trailer storage lot was an outlier of the Wilmot Creek retirement community, a big area of small, prefab houses with few trees. Torn-up fields were sprouting with the "suckers" from which more houses will grow: water, sewer, telephone, hydro and cable TV, pipes and wires, sticking up from the ground in a sparse irregular plantation.

The South Service Road doglegs out of the retirement subdivision past a stream which trickles out of a dense marsh of Hybrid Cattails, and then runs for a kilometre between the CN tracks and the Darlington hydro lines. Silverweed is the dominant herb along the roadside, its yellow blooms set off by this population's very silvery leaves. South of the road lay a narrow field of Soybeans and a ditch of Narrowleaf Cattail, and south of them, beyond the hydro lines the subdivision continues east to Cobbledick Road. There was Dogbane there, forming a surprisingly tall shrub-like thicket in the corner of a field near the tracks.

Wilmot Creek, Clarington, 10 September

As Fred walked the CN tracks from Port Darlington to meet us, Jennie, Bear and I walked toward the line of trees above Wilmot Creek, along a deeply rutted old field that grows Apple trees and Hawthorns in its hollows. A row of Oaks and Willow trees marks the rim of a lush, deep valley. The wire fence is mostly hidden in jungles of Goldenrod, Raspberry canes and billows of tall Pink Jewelweed, still in bloom. The track dips down and up, curving along the edge of a steep bank, and we look down to our left to see that the creek, deep and green, has meandered close to this side and then away again. The old field that lay on our right has given way to a broad crop of fuzzy-podded Soybeans.

We imagine the lake to be just beyond the crisp line of sky and field ahead, but feel we should go back to meet Fred. He is within sight of the parked truck when we get back, so we all drive in, and it proves a riskier business than I had supposed, as the ruts are alarming in places, and one dip is very abrupt. Curving from the Soy field at the ravine edge, the track enters a grove of Black Locust trees, with a spot for us to turn around before it slopes steeply down to the creek. We backed the truck into a gracefully gesturing Shadblow tree and shattered the back window of the cap into jewel-like fragments. Bear scrambled onto the cargo to escape from the explosion of glass and was trembling when we guided him through the shards to the ground.

The marshy mouth of Wilmot Creek sluices, clear and cold, into the lake through a gap in a gravelly bar. Down on the cobbly beach, we see that Locust trees from the grove above have slumped down the face of the gravelly bluff, some fallen and dead, but some gracefully arched and living. I sit on a low knee of the bluff to draw, with Bear tied to a drifted log. Jennie alternately tends her fire on the beach and watches fishermen casting lures into the marshy creek for Salmon, and Fred explores a short distance to the east along the narrow pebbly bluff-foot beach.

There were the remains of *Cambarus bartoni* crayfish in the drift and 30 Bank Swallow nest holes in the bluff face. A couple of easy-chair-size boulders stood offshore. The bluffs there are made of numerous kinds of sediment, arrayed in irregular layers: gravel in silty sand at the

bottom, lens-shaped inclusions of silt with a few embedded cobbles, old streambeds with boulders on the bottom grading up to finer gravel, cross-bedded sections of dune-laid sand, and on top a finely blocky or laminar silt-sand.

The line of drifted sticks and feathers on the beach included fish bones and lures, scraps of the creek-mouth salmonid fishery. Warm light from the setting sun slanted along the bluff, etching the textures of its bedded sediments, and picked out the green and white navigation light tower at Graham Creek to the east. Then a lead-grey cloud promptly extinguished the light effects. Clouds of caddis-flies hovered like a flurry of black snow.

Driving back along the west

side of Wilmot Creek, we pick deeply lobate leaves for Fred to print, from a dense, umbrella-shaped Hawthorn tree. I am impressed by the variety in leaf shape in Hawthorns, from smooth ovals to many-thumbed mitten shapes. Some bear long glossy red thorns and some are thornless.

Condylura cristata

Port Newcastle to 2.5 km east of Port Britain, 14 September

We stop at a gravel road T-intersection at the entrance to the sewage treatment plant, so Fred can get his gear together for the bicycle run to Port Hope. The tall Goldenrod is yellow-topped with bloom, aflutter with yellow and orange butterflies and hawking Dragonflies.

Fred set off on the road to the south, toward the Port Newcastle marina club, past a row of young Cedar with low scrub on either side. At the auditory survey site he followed a track down into the Graham Creek valley beside a patch of remnant deciduous forest. In May Fred and Lee Ann collected snails there and a Weasel ran under the truck. Since then everything has grown up into a tangle and a big Willow tree has fallen across the track. Fred met a toad on the path, saw a Leopard Frog and heard three more jumping in the tall grass. The wind had blown a blanket of minute green particles up to the end of the backwater arm of Graham Creek estuary, and big fish jumped from the still green water. Graham Creek was 4 m wide, with a rocky bottom farther upstream where he crossed it on Mill Street.

He picked up a Starnose Mole dead on the road a few metres west of the bridge. He found two moles today ("It was a two-mole day.") and since this first one was in excellent condition I have drawn it at camp in Port Darlington while its nose is still fresh and pink, by the light of a 12-volt trouble lamp. It is an adult, 180 mm total length, with a white tuft on the extreme tip of the tail.

He looked for crayfish in Graham Creek, finding abundant *Orconectes propinquus* under small stones and also Raccoon tracks in mud along the creek. Then he made a run down Mill Street, through a residential woodland dominated by mature Maples and began to note road-kills: three Toads, one Garter Snake and two Leopard Frogs.

The Bond Head parkette is a small lawn-park at the mouth of Graham Creek, above a sand and pebble beach. As Fred paused for lunch a cold fog wafted off the lake. He noted that some of the rocks offshore bore the felty coat of algae that indicates high nutrient levels in the water. He also found it curious that the beach shelter had an open, latticework roof. Continuing east past small cottagy houses, down past a beach-access parkette and up along the lake where he found a tall stand of Lambsquarters growing on a steep bare slope between the road and the lake. Cold lake air and warm land air alternated in buffets under the hazy sun as he cycled east past bluff-edge houses and Soya and Alfalfa fields on the plain above Bond Head.

He crossed a hayfield to the brink of the bluff, where red-leaved Poison Ivy was scattered among the grass. The horizon was lost in haze, but the sun was warm at the top of the dissected and gullied bluffs. The face of the bluff was tufted with Rose bushes and Coltsfoot greened the narrow silt fans at the bottom.

Turning back to the road, he was astonished to see a pair of Whimbrels in a hayfield. One doesn't look for Curlews so high above the lake and so far from the shore. These were so heavy-bodied that he thought they were ducks at first, before they called and he saw their bills. They were too short-billed for Long-bill Curlews, and didn't show any cinnamon in flight when he put them up. They circled out over the lake and then around to the north. Still watching for the Whimbrels, he paused on a bridge while a fast train on the CN tracks and two long slow trains on the CP tracks passed beneath. He stood there for a long time, mesmerized by the hope of Curlews and the passing of so much heavy metal and noise.

Then the road ran through typical Ontario farmland with scattered wild Lilacs in the fencerows, hay, Corn and Soya fields, Apple orchards and irri-gated Cauliflower fields. The monotony of farm fields was punctuated by occasional glimpses of the lake to the south. He then crossed the tracks south towards Bouchette Point and in valley woods found our first Alternate-leaved Dogwood of the trip, a 7 m tree leaning toward the roadway, bearing a profusion of small dark blue berries. Also along the road were stands of Black Elderberry, their panicles only sparsely sprinkled with fruit, perhaps due to poor pollination, as we have seen all the way from Toronto. He coasted past Paper Birches to a streamside flat dominated by Wild Cucumber and Ostrich Fern. The clear gravelly trickle was too small for crayfish. Large Ironwood trees and some picturesquely-twisted Beech and Black Willow date from a time when this area was grazed woodland or pasture.

Then he rolled past roadsides of Lilacs, over a great road-slaughter of big black crickets, and down into a valley bordered by neat stands of Cedars. At the bridge over a muddy rocky brook, he found *Physa* snails on the silty algal fringes of stones, and the crayfish *Orconectes propinquus* beneath them.

The next little rocky brook, Port Granby Creek, ran past Cedars in pastures and house yards and was clearer than the last stream. Under rocks downstream of the bridge, there were lots of sculpins and darters and *Physa* snails, but no crayfish, which left him wondering about the relationships among these under-stone species. Up out of the Port Granby valley the Lakeshore road continued past Corn fields, and then the fenced-in lawn that surrounds lagoons for treating radioactive water from Ontario Hydro. He pedalled past Cedar woodland with a lovely view north over grassy ridges, and then through a little Cattail marsh in the hollow of Cedar woods flagged with White Pine, and finally up to the road along the Durham-Northumberland county boundary.

This road led north to our "CNCP" auditory station at the paired tracks, a marsh surrounded by mixed woods and Cedar-Poplar second growth. The water level in the marsh was low, with turtle tracks in the mud by the road culvert. Two Painted Turtles were basking in an excavated pond beside a house. A scan of the road for fragments turned up pieces of another Painted Turtle, a Garter Snake, a scrap of Green Frog and a Wood Frog.

S FRED STOOD, writing notes, a Snapping Turtle headed across the road. Since he couldn't pick it up by the short stub of its tail, he dribbled it across the pavement with his feet, out of the way of a passing schoolbus and home-from-work CN trucks. Just as he was ready to leave at 16:32, the few high, scratchy Spring Peeper calls he had noticed on his arrival picked up and became regular. This is a herpetologically diverse and valuable place: six species found in late summer without even leaving the road!

Fred cycled back south to the Lakeshore Road and continued west through Wesleyville, a small community with a brick schoolhouse and an 1860 Wesley church: a comfortable place where wild shrubs, flowering Goldenrod and Asters grow unmown beneath grand old Sugar Maples. In the old fields near the Wesleyville Thermal Generating Station, he found a multitude of seed-like *Pupilla muscorum* snails on the underside of a piece of plywood thrown down in roadside Crown Vetch. A clear sandy-bottomed stream flowed from an ungrazed meadow towards the Hydro plant.

Continuing past farms and residences, Fred found himself in rolling land where Port Britain appeared to the southeast as an island of trees among the fields; there is no village-like concentration of houses along Lakeshore Road here, as most of the houses are in the woods to the south. As he approached Port Britain Creek, Green Frogs jumped in, familiar splashes that we haven't heard much this summer. The creek is clear, a few metres wide and half a metre deep with a sand and rock bottom, running parallel to the road along a lawn. There were many *Orconectes propinquus*, a few *Cambarus bartoni* under big stones and in burrows, and he saw what could have been a small *Orconectes virilis*. If there are three species of crayfish here, that's more than we have seen in a single stream all summer.

At the corner of Haskill and Lakeshore roads stands a big old Yellow Birch. By its maple-like bark, low stout crown and branches dying back, Fred thought at first that it was an ailing

member of the Sugar Maples that
line the road to the east and
north. When roadside Sugar Maples were planted for sugar
production, perhaps this
Birch was mistaken for
a Maple, or perhaps it
was intentionally
planted there as a special tree.
Their battered crowns show that all of
them are struggling for survival now.
Old age and acid rain, and perhaps
other factors too, are taking their toll.
To the north is a grassed drumlin.
Abandoned on one slope is an elegant
Victorian frame house, long bare of
paint, as silent about its stories as the
Yellow Birch.

Alternate-
leaved
Dogwood
*Cornus
alternifolia*

Four hundred metres farther on, as
he was picking up the second Starnose
Mole of the day, Jennie and I pass him
in the truck. We stop to take him and
his bike aboard and continue to a spot
just past Brands Creek, where I recog-
nise the view that I'd admired this
spring, a blue triangle of the lake
through a gap in the old Grand Trunk
railway embankment. I still want to
paint it, but now the light's failing, so
we head back to camp.

**2.5 km east of Port Britain,
17 September**
It is 19:30. I have just finished my
painting of the abandoned railway embankment beyond a field full of Dogwood, Goldenrod and Aster. Monarch
Butterflies are coming inland from the
shore, fluttering and lilting over the
Goldenrod, crossing the Lakeshore
Road against the stiffening breeze.

Some are as
high as 10 m above
me, setting their wings
and coasting a little when
they come to a lull in the
wind. There must be a certain
place where they "camp" for the night.
They've been coming this way steadily,
four or five visible at most times, since
about 17:30. Sometimes they chase
each other flitting and looping, their
motion haphazard and flippant, but
when I see them work so determinedly
against the wind, I have new respect for
their strength and purpose.

Crickets sing stridently in the ditch
and a dragonfly courses back and forth,
ignoring the passing Monarchs. The
sun is setting, and after I write a few
more notes, we must go to meet Fred.

Port Hope, 17 September
As I painted the Grand Trunk embankment, Fred biked east along Lakeshore
Road to Port Hope. He scanned the
road for scraps, picking up a road-
killed Toad, a Green Frog and a Leopard Frog. Then where the road dips un-

der the CN and CP tracks in close underpasses, he walked the bike south along the edge of a field of ripening Soybeans, past lobed-leaved Hawthorn Buckthorn, Sumac, Wild Raisin and Apple, all in fruit. Monarchs and Dragonflies animated the air above the Soybeans as he walked the field edge down to the lake. The surf rolled in like a truck, on a beach like a highway of loose round gravel. Ruddy-fruited Hawthorns fronted the slumping-over brink of the bluffs. At the mouth of Baluchs Creek he found no crayfish or snails in the stream, which may dry up in summer. A few white Cedars have established themselves in the gully at its mouth.

Back on Lakeshore Road at the grassy railway embankment, a large

derpasses, then continued northeast past Corn and Soy fields, noting another Garter Snake, with the road heavily spotted with the death marks of Crickets and caterpillars.

As he entered Port Hope's residential woodland he turned south past Norway Maple woods and a golf course and then south and east along the edge of a bluff, past elegant large houses among mature trees. He saw two Grey Squirrels, one of them black-coated. The woods that run down the slopes of the bluffs are dominated by Norway Maple, Horse Chestnuts and Black Locust, as if they were seeded by exotic street trees after all native trees had been removed.

He then rolled east down a steep slope, zigged south on John Street past small brick houses, zagged east at a big chemical plant, past a former industrial mooring site converted into a

The Grand Trunk railway bed

Apple tree gave wonderfully sweet-sour red fruit. He thought it would be worthy of founding a cultivar, but when the Apples were brought back, they quickly turned mealy.

He found the remains of Toad and Garter Snake between the railway un-

playpen for sailboats, and out along a narrow gravel road to the open lake at the harbour. The piers along the west bank of the mouth of the Ganaraska River were lined with the cars and folding chairs of hopeful salmon fishermen placidly whipping the water.

On a tiny beach tucked in between seawalls he found nine tiny *Physa* snail shells. A banded Trumpeter Swan stood beside a boy who alternately threw bread and stones at Gulls and Mallards. Signs in the lot to the north warn of soil contamination by non-radioactive materials, of buried water mains, and that fish should not be consumed without consulting established standards of contamination.

Crossing the river on the first bridge, he headed south again along the east bank of the river to a sand-beach urban parkette, picking a crayfish claw and old worn shells, mostly fingernail clams, from a fine drift at the base of the pier. He passed a neighbourhood of small lakefront houses and then the trail became a wood-bordered gravel path across a broad slope of Tansies and little planted pines between industrial buildings and the concrete-slab beach.

The path continued, Willow-shaded, along a coarse gravel bar that separates the lake from a wide marsh of Hybrid Cattails, variegated by Water Hemlock and Water Smartweed. He passed a green wooden viewing platform and crossed the metre-wide mouth of Gage Creek where it runs out over the algae-felted cobble beach, noting "a tranquil rippling scene" with two Killdeer, a peep and a Blackbelly Plover. He continued east, pushing his bike through beach sand after the Waterfront trail had turned north past the Sewage Treatment Plant.

He followed a narrow path through Willow thickets between the pastel sunset waves and the Cattail marsh. He caught a green female Leopard Frog in a rut in the path, and then walked and rode along the narrow sand and gravel beach to our auditory station. There he crossed the CN tracks and rode north along the access road to Hwy 2, where he waited in the sunset on a pile of concrete median dividers for Jennie and me.

West Beach, Port Darlington, Clarington, 15 September

This is the last day at our West Beach camp. Fred brought a Herring Gull in from the beach yesterday. Newly dead, its eyes were still bright and yellow. It was just finishing its juvenile moult, so the head is

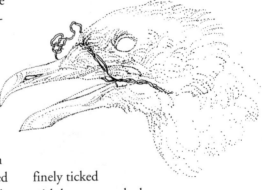

finely ticked with brown-streaked feathers on new white plumage, the back and wings a delicate pearl grey.

We didn't notice the cause of its death until this morning, the fine clear snarl of monofilament fishing line that encircled its upper mandible and passed around its neck. If the nylon line didn't choke it, it had certainly starved it.

AWSON Marsh, north of our camp, is part of the conservation area of the Central Lake Ontario Conservation Authority. An old road leads into the centre of the Cattail marsh, along the west bank of Bowmanville Creek, from our auditory station at West Beach Road. Fred went in there two days ago and saw Snapping Turtle eggs beside predator-opened nests and Beaver bite-marks on small Black Locust trees on the fill-built bank above the creek channel. He saw two Leopard Frogs and five juvenile Toads. Two of these were under boards on the narrow sandy creek-edge, two were active and one was in the mouth of a Garter Snake.

This morning Jennie and I went north on the road along the marsh, toward the impressive creek-side line of old Willow trees. The old road, now closed to traffic, runs along the creek from a little parking lot. As soon as we come beneath the Willow trees we are met by a riot of autumn wildflowers. Billowing clouds of Pink Jewelweed rise to shoulder and head height. The flamboyance of their pink display is softened by the lavender colour of New England Asters, set off by Goldenrod, and then sparkled against green foliage by yellow daisy-like *Bidens* and orange Jewelweed. Jennie notices that some of the Pink Jewelweed flowers here are white.

The view down the sandy roadway is enchanting. The tall Willows lean this way and that in graceful groups. To the west they lean over the marsh Cat-

tails, and Redwing Blackbirds "chick" somewhere in their upper branches. To the east they lean over cloudy-green creek water, very still today. Single spikes of closely packed white-hooded blossoms stand at the feet of some of the Willows, the strange-flowered plant called Turtlehead.

Stepping quietly, we pass a sleeping fisherman who entrusts his rod to a forked stick in the bank. A sodden marshmallow glimmers below where his line enters the water. Soon we find ourselves across the creek from the boat launch and arrive at a wooden observation tower. From the top we look over the marsh and back along the Willows, taking in a broad view of the harbour and the line of cottages along the beach, with our little white trailer and red truck tucked in at the end. On the centre post of the roofed top deck, posters display the history of Port Darlington, which we read before climbing back down. Then Jennie rides her bike while I jog, back along the peninsula of dry land through the marsh and back down the road to camp, in time to batten down for our move to Grafton.

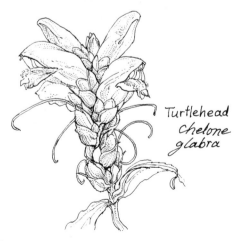

Turtlehead
Chelone glabra

11

Grafton Creek Camp

Moving camp to Grafton has been our longest leap between camps. Nawautin Shores at the mouth of Grafton Creek, is a property of rich second growth, Cedar and wetland, being developed both for residential use and public wildland.

Port Hope to Carr Marsh, Hamilton Twp., 21 September

Jennie and I walk across the railway tracks from the "east of Port Hope" auditory station, where Fred had pushed his bike up from the beach on 17 September. The sun glares through a thin haze that masks the horizon with a bright pink veil, and the lake laps gently, crisscrossed by dimples and smooth ripples. Fred has returned to the truck, leaving us to walk the beach to Carr Marsh where he will walk down to the lake to meet us.

Gull tracks make a pattern of diamond-shaped trademarks in the sand, and the drift line is mostly poplar leaves and gull feathers. A large dark Goose stands alone 100 m up the beach and stretches one leg behind luxuriously. Thick shrubs of Willow grow in sweeping gestures over the sand, reminding me of Sagebrush. Stooping, we puzzle over a line of strange footprints in the sand that look as if they were made by a tiny feather-footed

Chicken, dragging its rear claws. Fred says he saw some of these too, and we conclude that they are Toad prints.

We cross the low dunes to see the pond that's marked on the map as lying between beach and railroad tracks. In the shade of a Willow tree, a bank of heart-shaped Bindweed leaves tangle over the broadleaved grasses, one flower open like a small candy-striped Morning Glory. The pond is shallow and about 50 m across. Little round Frogbit leaves float near this shore, and minnow movements dimple the surface of the clear water. Turning, I frighten a large frog from grassy sand into the dense bank vegetation. Grasshoppers pop dryly in the yellow grasses as I shuffle for more frogs. Fine parallel lines indicate where perhaps a beetle walked across the sand. Jennie shows me the empty shell of a glossy dark brown chrysalis, probably carried here by a mouse to eat in the open.

We come to a place where the lake has some time ago broken through the dunes, and where Geese come down from the beach to the still pond waters. Several unseen frogs plop into the water from the willow-bushy bank as we approach. Tiny water beetles shift about in little jerks on the bottom. A minnow comes to investigate the disturbance in the sediment as I take the water temperature. Jennie collects some *Stagnicola elodes* snails from the sandy bottom of the "goose ramp." Farther down the beach, black-winged Caddisflies dance in rhythmic circles and figure-eights, tracing invisible "Trichopta-script" back and forth above the sun warmed sand.

An old beach Willow makes a picturesque dragon-arch half-way out across the beach, bristling a crest of living and dead branches against the bright sky, and shading a green "treasure" of Coltsfoot

Oenothera oakesiana, a special lakeshore primrose

Lobelia siphalitica

beneath the arching "neck." Jennie collects the head of a freshly gull-cleaned Sucker from the wave's edge.

Now the beach runs along a stretch of bushy old fields, toward a gentle point. There a grove of young White Cedar holds back a high drift of round beach pebbles. On the point itself there is more drift – fragments of clam shell, a block of painted wood, a red shotgun shell and a deflated bunch of birth-day balloons. A single Jewelweed stands alone on the upper beach, decked out with orange flowers. Dark "sleeves" of aphids on two of its branches are being tended by busy black ants, and a La-dybird beetle with 16 black spots sleeps on a leaf.

We pass a burlap-walled duck blind. As I stand to take notes, my writing hand is visited by a mating pair of black caddisflies. Tail to tail, they poise, wings overlapping, antennae waving in the wind, and fuzzy palps neatly curled in front of their heads.

We round the next headland to a wild-looking cedar-lined cove. Tall White Cedars, fallen into the water across the narrow beach, make an impenetrable tangle, so Jennie and I press into the woods. I worry about the time, as we should soon be meeting Fred at the Carr Marsh, a discouraging distance along the shore of the sketch he traced from the topo map. The for-est is beautiful inside, dim and spooky with graceful lichen-stained trunks curving up in intimate groups from an undulating floor of litter-blanketed Cedar roots. The lake must have washed through here years ago, exposing the forest's underground parts. Stray streaks of low sunlight make orange paths across the Cedar leaf litter and up smooth trunks. Lady Fern mists the floor with soft green, and splashes of tall Jewelweed grow, unflowered.

We skirt a grassy swale, where a patch of strange-flowered Wood-nettles grows. The ground is moist among Poplars, and the Alders become so thick that we decide to force our way out to the beach, through a Dogwood thicket and over a scramble of bleached Willow trunks. There we meet Fred, wading toward us around the roots of fallen Willows. He had seen us against the horizon just before we entered the Cedar woods. We head back along a diffi- cult

stretch of cobble beach, with big Black Willows in and out of the water. One Willow stands, splaying its roots out into a pavement of loose flat beach cobbles at the edge of an Alder thicket.

Aphid honeydew collects on the leaves of the Willows and falls like rain drops, wetting the stones beneath the trees. Flowers of Great Lobelia glimmer purple from a shady depression, and I pick a plant to put in my vasculum. Enjoying the sweet lemon scent of one of the last yellow flowers atop an evening primrose stalk, I decide to pick it as well.

An impenetrable tangle of Alder creeps down to the beach among

Canada
Wood-nettle
Laportea canadensis

124

the branches of a downed lake
Willow. We waded beneath
the branches of one, and then
walked along those of an-
other. Above the water
the grassy pelt of its
rootwad holds a gar-
den of *Polygonum,*
Vetch and yellow
Bidens. Just at sunset
we see the open marsh
ahead to the left, and a
gentle curve of pebbly beach.
The upper beach of smooth multicoloured stones is like a precious garden.
Little plantings of fine mossy *Sedum* ar-
range themselves with misty-leaved
Cockleburr and rosy-catkinned
Knotweed among graceful curves of
driftwood.

A line of dead *Scirpus* rhizomes is
exposed a metre from the water's gravelly edge, 10 cm above the present lake
level. All along this beach we have
found these rootstocks in the drift,
though we saw no living Bulrush plants
in the marsh or lake. Here we find
their source eroding out above a layer
of big flat cobbles and below a bed of
smaller gravel, and wonder how long
ago they lived here.

The sky and the lake are purple pink
behind us in the west, and the light all
around us is becoming violet. Two red
lights on one of two radio towers glow
above the trees to the northeast, beside
the nearly-full moon. We quicken our
pace, anxious to get back before dark.

The Cattail marsh has a border of
Burr Reed here, the leaves rusty tipped
in this late season. Now with beds of

Scirpus root.

Nightshade,
Xanthium and
Evening Primrose,
the upper beach
crowds out the Burr
Reed, and the tall Cat-
tails of the marsh come
right up to the pebbles of
the beach. We walk along
an arched highway of
beach between the marsh
and the lapping lake. Grasshoppers are singing in the
moonlit dusk. A graceful "oasis"
of six young Willow trees stands in the
sand, just down from the crest of pebbles, and another Willow lies uprooted
nearby. The wide area of shoal water
out to Peters Rock must protect this
shore from violent waves, allowing the
growth of the trees that eventually fall
down over the beach. We can see its
navigation light, a little over a kilometre offshore.

UST AT DARK we repack our gear, stopping at the place where Fred has stashed a cotton Tilley Hat he picked up on the beach for Jennie, the only human artifact we have seen all along this wild shore since we left the Cedar cove. Now we strike north into Carr Marsh, west of the creek mouth, with the red lights of the radio towers ahead and to the right, stepping along through a deep soft bed of tall, bushy, *Calamagrostis* grass. We take long steps over partly lodged grasses, as if we were walking on loosely piled hay. The grasses swish and rustle as we brush along a wandering path that is narrow in places and then widens out, as if opening into Deer beds.

Single Cattails stand tall and flexibly strong, their heads high above our own. Even the grass is above our heads, especially in the middle of the marsh, where the Cattails form a denser stand, supporting the grass. We feel very small in the dark, like Fleas in the coat of a Dog within this rustling pelt of the earth. Jennie often trips as she bounds over grass stems lodged at knee height, though there are no hummocks or snags until we come out through a thigh-high sea of shorter grass to the area beneath the radio towers. Here brush has been cleared and Fred warns us of hidden stumps. He has a light, but it only illuminates the nearby grass, and moonlight gives him a better feel for the vague path we follow. We come out through low Dog-

wood scrub to a gravel road, which leads to the railway tracks and the truck at 20:21, parked at the Carr Marsh auditory station on Bob Carr Road. The full moon, orange and perfectly framed over the railway tracks, is centred between rounded black crowns of trees on either side.

Cobourg, 24 September

At 06:00 Fred awoke and heard scattered Peepers calling, which increased to a sparse chorus and then stopped as the sky lightened with dawn. At this point fusillades of shotgun fire began from the east, evidently announcing the beginning of the hunting season. Crows called as if in alarm, flocks of Chickadees started to forage through the alders, whispering their "dee-dee" calls and a Song Sparrow began to sing.

In the early afternoon he set out on a bicycle trip to Cobourg and back, to close the gap between Carr Marsh and beach walks he had already made east and west of this camp.

Past Barnumhouse Creek, Lakeshore Road ended at a gated track to cottages, so Fred took Archer Road north to Hwy 2, finding a snake which he hailed as our first non-Garter Snake, a Redbelly crushed on the north slope of the bridge that crosses the CN and CP tracks.

Where Hwy 2 crosses a tiny unnamed brook, black Squirrels were active on the campus lawns, and drake and hen Mallard were sitting by the stream. Hwy 2 took him through a residential area, the elegant old-brick downtown, the Conservation Area lawns and the strip with its vast parking lots.

He left Hwy 2 where the trail route follows Rogers Road south between old fields soon to be developed into a "community combining tradition and innovation for a quality lifestyle." Following Carlisle and Ewing, he came to a little springfed pond in the housing subdivision, a place where utility connections were installed and a cellar hole dug in clayey sand, only to have springs burst out of the ground and form a pond of clear water. A big frog jumped into the water when Fred walked around the pond but did not re-emerge for identification. The only conspicuous plants were a few stalks of Cattail and the floating-leaved *Ranaculus sceleratus* with tiny yellow blooms, said to be named Cursed Buttercup for its growth in "vile places." Sixteen Bank Swallow nest holes looked out from a wall of sand behind the weedy excavated area of the pond.

He came down through older subdivisions to Monks Cove Park commanding a calm grey vista over the lake above the massive armouring of the shore. Fred zigzagged down a path to the gravel beach, which runs east in a smooth curve. A ball-obsessed Dog insisted that he pitch for it, chasing a tennis ball over the sparse trampled beach-drift of algal felt.

When he got back up to the bike he found that its overloaded basket rack had broken. He lashed the rods together with twine, and wobbled along King Street. Standing on the bridge over Cobourg Brook, he watched a

Kingfisher flying down the path of the shallow creek as it flowed through a residential area toward the lake. Fred went downstream too, along the estuarine creek to its mouth, through the Balsam-Poplar lawns of the Cobourg Peace Park. An olive-coloured salmonid, about 70 cm long, had been caught by boys, who seemed not to know what to do with it. A man who walked up and viewed it didn't seem to be able to help them. The creek was lined with fishers trying to achieve similar success.

It was getting late for his return, as the days are not as long as they were when we began in July. He came down to the beach west of Cobourg Harbour, and walked from the Villa Saint Joseph Retreat Centre to the boulder pier west of Cobourg Harbour. The beach is fine gravel, but above it is a wide sand flat where Sea-Rocket is the dominant herb, some blooming, others in seed, the fleshy leaves a tasty bitter nibble. A dwarfed Sunflower, only 25 cm tall, stood gone to seed, but bearing a tiny secondary blossom, in the drift line. We have seen a number of these dwarves, probably sprouted from birdseed, on Lake Ontario beaches, but this is the smallest. In muddy duckweed-tumbled beach-drift at the base of the pier, Fred picked up a few scraps of crayfish and many old mollusc shells, including European Faucet Snail, Great Lakes Horn Snail, Three-keeled Valve Snail and *Physa* pond snails.

He crossed over the base of the pier to Cobourg Harbour, and around the quiet harbour basin on a bricked walk.

He passed a Cormorant and flocks of Mallards on a floating mat of automobile tires, the mast thicket of a small marina, and a wide paved pier east of the harbour, while large fish swirled in the water with occasional explosive splashes.

To the east the trail route runs through Victoria Park, with its RV camp, wide lawns and sand beach. Fred followed it along the shore past small houses and the huge batteries of night-sports lights in Donegan Park, which adjoins the grounds of a water filtration plant. From the bridge over the narrow ravine of Brook Road Creek, he watched another Kingfisher in along-the-creek flight, and then cycled through a small-house residential area to Hwy 2 at Maplewood Drive.

He headed east along the torn-up highway shoulders in deepening dusk. Nine kilometres and a harrowing hour later he heard the first Peepers of the evening from Lakeshore Road at Grafton Creek. At camp, autumn calling by Peepers continued all night, and, at 06:28 a distant Great Horned Owl was hooting by dawn- and moonlight.

Victoria Park, Cobourg, 1 October

A view of the lake between the wet black trunks of willows and the wooden pillars of a "shelter" with a lattice roof. Two huge Cottonwood trees dwarf the little structure with their elephantine trunks of grooved corky bark. An elegant brick sidewalk runs past this little building and a high concrete curb steps down onto the deep sand of a wide beach. Fred, Jennie and Bear are looking for drift and exploring the Cobourg Harbour pier while I sit to draw through the windshield of the truck, to shelter from the steady drizzle and occasional fit of rain.

Farther to the right, big frothing waves rush along the breakwater pier, arching their crests right up to the top of the white-painted railing, and combing their manes up in flying fingers against the corrugated steel plate of the pier wall. We wait, entranced, watching for the next big wave. Wave watching is a special kind of meditation. It clears one's mind of everything but rapt anticipation of the power and beauty of the next big one.

My drawing finished, we walk along

Victoria Park

the beach and down the east side of the broad pier to watch the chugging rush of the big crests from above. Two wave-trains, the incoming swells, and their reflections, combine to form momentary mountains a little way off the pier. The big crests that rush along the corrugated wall make repeated puffing splashes almost in our faces. Here the water is a greyish tan, full of stirred sediment, while on the harbour side of the pier it is a deep clear green. The L-shaped notch where the breakwater curves away from the end of the pier focuses the slosh, cannonading it up into fountains that dash down onto the asphalt and run back into the lake. Fred jumped back as one of the "big ones" exploded upward in his face.

A long line of yachts is perched on steel scaffolding at the base of pier. A man with a long hose directs a fanned spray of hot water along the keel of one of the boats, erasing the dark skin of algae from its blue hull with each stroke. A truck backs a long trailer in, to take another yacht away for winter storage.

Barnumhouse-Grafton creeks, Haldimand, 19 September

At 15:00 Jennie and I left Fred at the township fishing access at the mouth of Barnumhouse Creek to walk back to camp, before we continue to Cobourg. It's a lazy beginning-of-fall day. The sun is still warm and most leaves still green, though some are starting to fall. Alders and Dogwood are ragged from leaf loss, Orange Jewelweed is bursting seeds, and *Clematis* vines are drying their silky greenish ribbon-clusters,

bursting them into billows of grey fluff. The wind is driving surf onto the beaches. Some of the strongest waves push water back up the creeks, turning them grey-green and placid.

Several Leopard Frogs escaped through trampled tall grass as Fred worked his way through a brushy area at the mouth of the creek which runs fast but shallow over its coarse gravel bar. Stream-spawning salmonids must have a hard time getting over these bars, and the old Atlantic Salmon fishery must have concentrated at places like this.

Then Fred stepped onto the beach, in the full blast of the wind, and his hat blew off. The sand and till bluffs there are four or five metres high. Walking at the bottom along the gravel beach, he picked a few crayfish claws from scattered drifts of old sticks. Above him ran a straggling row of Bank Swallow holes just below the lip of the bluff, most in sand, but often up in the browned B-horizon of the soil.

A little farther east the bluff is higher, and even if one cannot read the details, one can see that a complex story of lakes and glaciers is told on its face. The lower 10 m is a messy unsorted till of dark limestone gravel and cobbles and scattered igneous boulders embedded in hard pale sandy silt, evidently lying just as the ice sheet left it. Above this lies a narrow bed of massive silt which grades eastward into a deformed twisted wood-grain of thin layers, perhaps deposited in a lake and deformed by post-glacial slumping. Above that sits a metre or so of laminated gravels, probably fossil beaches, up to the sparse sod. The till of the bluff has collapsed onto the present gravel beach in big blocks, forming ramparts that sheltered Fred as he wrote. The waves were murky with their work of sorting the sediments, and a "force six" wind rolled whitecaps across the lake to a clear horizon.

A kilometre east of the creek mouth, the bluffs are taller and quite vertical, the massive till like towering concrete walls, and the main sign of human influence was garden waste. Grass clippings, brush and whole cut trees had been thrown over the edge onto the gravel beach. In places the garden waste was caught under slumps of till, and "fossilized" at beach level.

Moving east, he found the bluffs highly structured with cross-bedded till, sand and gravel. They were riddled with Bank Swallow and Kingfisher nest burrows, and diminished in height until they were gone, and a field of blooming wild Carrots came right down to the beach. In the lee of a Scots Pine caddisflies formed fluttering swarms like black snow at the edge of the beach by the Ukrainian summer camp.

On 6 May Fred and Lee Ann had driven down to the beach there and walked east to

long, hairy "feeler" mouth-parts that fold up under the head——

A Trichopteran adult, "hatched" out of the lake.

dark red eyes

pair of smaller fringed wings hidden underneath outer wings—

the mouth of Grafton Creek, as a strong wind drove in a 70-cm surf, milky with sediment. They picked up scattered crayfish and snail shells and were puzzled by the bulldozing and little bridges at the mouth of the creek. This was the developing wetland of Nawautin, which is now as familiar as home. They found a fine skim drift of small snail shells, blown into a flat area at the mouth of the creek. The aquatic snails identified from their drift samples are *Aplexa hypnorum, Fossaria modicella, Fossaria truncatula, Gyraulus circumstriatus, Helisoma trivolvis, Planorbula armigela, Stagnicola elodes* and the land snails *Vertigo ovata* and *Oxyloma.*

Today as Fred came along the beach, below woods of Balsam Poplar and planted pines, the sparse summer drift yielded only a few old chelipeds, and the surf had built the creek-mouth bar into a flat berm of sand.

Grafton Creek to Wicklow boat-launch, 18 September
While Bob Marshall, our host at Nawautin, took Jennie and me to the dedication of the Wicklow Beach Boat launch, Fred left camp on foot to walk the shore and meet us there. From the east end of Nawautin, he passed through a fencerow of Ash, Wild Raisin and Hawthorn, to the wide sweep of the Ash-lined beach. Looking west before he set out, he saw shining bluffs, the white towers of the chemical plant at Cobourg, and, westernmost, the single stack of the Wesleyville Thermal Generating Station.

The gravel and sand kilometre east to Chub Point, past a row of beach houses, showed a drift of mostly sticks and feathers, with one colourful clump of ribbons and burst balloons from "Greektown on the Danforth" painted with profiles of the Toronto skyline. As he rounded Chub Point he noticed bright yellow Bigtooth Aspen leaves in the drift and, looking up, saw a grove of Aspens among the Cottonwoods.

The pebble beach was grooved as if by successive storms or motor vehicle tracks. Flat limestone bedrock just at the water level extended to an offshore rock. Near the mouth of Shelter Valley Creek, two Leopard Frogs jumped from a clay-bottomed pocket in the gravel. The creek drains a small marsh surrounded by Purple Loosestrife and a tall stand of Arrowhead. The tiny floating plants *Wolffia columbiana* and *Lemna minor* formed a dense thick duckweed blanket on the open water. The creek flows out at the east end of the marsh, a strong knee-deep stream of clear water over a gravel bar. One fisherman was plying his silent sport as Fred passed.

After nearly a kilometre of easy walking below slumping bluffs, he came to a new grey house, with a bull-dozed slope running right down to the water and a dense stand of Cedar eroding into the lake from 4-5-m bluffs. Then there was a stretch where the bluffs were armoured by boulders, tree stumps and concrete liberally dumped from bluff-top Apple orchards. On the bluff face, Grapes and Wild Cucumber draped over Manitoba Maple, Nettles,

Hawthorn and other plants in a dense wall of vegetation which kept Fred right down at the water's edge.

Past a little point of piled boulders and concrete slabs, he followed a narrow gravel beach below the open Poplar woodland of a summer camp, where he picked up a few scraps of drifted *Orconectes propinquus* claws and carapace, and a chunk of the toothrow of a Whitetail Deer.

On the beach bar that fronts the marsh at the mouth of Wicklow Creek, he found fragments and parts of four valves of *Anadonta grandis*, our first concentration of fresh unionid shells. Then at the creek mouth, two juvenile Toads were both in the same hole under a plywood scrap on upper beach sand. On the bar that blocks the creek, he found curled craps of egg shell and one nearly hatched Snapping Turtle embryo in nests opened by Skunks or Raccoons. On his approach to the edge of the bar-blocked creek mouth, he scared up four juvenile Leopard Frogs and one juvenile Wood Frog. As the dominant frog of both the Boreal Forest and mature deciduous forest, this small brown frog with the dark eye mask and white lip stripe is the most poignant *Rana* to meet along the lakeshore. We didn't hear calling west of Ajax, and found summer frogs at only three sites along the waterfront.

A mowed path runs along the beach bar past a rich wetland, and Fred followed it to a sandy patch littered with more remains of rifled turtle nests. The creek channel through the marsh was dense with Frogbit leaves like miniature lily pads, and many emergent plants, dominated by Broadleaf Cattail and Purple Loosestrife. The path continued through Balsam Poplar woods between the wetland and the beach, and then through a Willow woods, to come out on the beach where a patch of woods was bulldozed. To the east, the beachside woods were occupied by lightly-used commercial campsites, and had he looked far along the beach he would have seen the grey rock-armoured flanks of the new Wicklow boat launch, and perhaps Jennie and me on the beach, watching for him to appear.

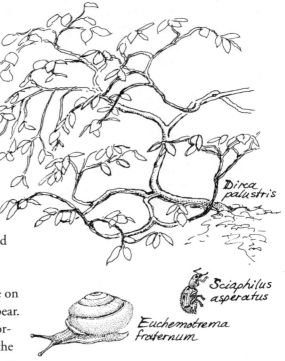

Dirca palustris

Sciaphilus asperatus

Euchemotrema fraternum

That night we heard a Whippoorwill calling, just as the frogs do in the fall, only briefly, in the bright full moon.

Peters Woods, north of Centreton, Haldimand, 26 September

Bob Marshall led us north of our planned route to an old growth forest on the Oak Ridges Moraines north of Centreton, where kames, or hills of till were left behind when the glaciers melted. This place, called Peters Woods, is well inland from the lake, and offers us a taste of what relatively undisturbed woods are like away from the physical and cultural effects of the lake front.

From the parking lot, under a dark woods of tall Maple and Basswood, we walk through a narrow space in a Cedar rail fence, and enter an old field growing in wild with young Basswoods and White Pines.

Our path turns left along the edge of a Maple woods, and entering it, we move through a glow of living green, traced down with the inky lines of young wet-barked trunks. As the trees become larger and the forest more spacious beneath the mature canopy, we can see, past a columnar Sugar Maple without a top, into a valley of treespace. We pass Birches whose pink under-bark blushes through the wet chalky outer bark. A huge Basswood trunk curves smoothly, its top lost above the lower canopy. Jays call and raindrops patter from leafy boughs above onto a sprinkle of golden leaf litter.

Directed by a yellow arrow atop a post, we step carefully down the valley slope. Anise Root stands beside the footbridge at the bottom, smooth-stemmed plants with ferny tomato-like leaves. High above the leaves, at the ends of a spidery splay of dry-branched flower stalks, hang lance-shaped seeds like little black fishes.

The sandy creek bed is dry, with Jewelweed and lacy yellow-green Bulblet Ferns on its banks. Maidenhair Ferns beside the path swirl crescents of fringed, blue-green pinnae on glossy black stems. A Beech tree, fallen across the trail, has been cut into sections and left to rot and feed the forest. A Coral Hedgehog fungus drips bunches of fine fingers like ivory stalactites from a broken branch end, and the smooth, rain-darkened bole of the Beech stretches back across ferns, Horsetail and seedling Maples to the rearing crest of its big flat rootwad.

Christmas Fern

Polystichum acrostichoides

The trail follows the creek at the top edge of its valley, and then strikes off away from it through level forest. Nuthatches are holding "anka"-ing contests somewhere in the canopy. Fred and Jennie encircle the girth of a big sloping Maple tree with their arms. Fred opens part of a rolling log and exposes a dainty, shiny Redback Salamander. Jennie examines a spiny Beechnut capsule, finding a triangular nut in each side of the double, four-bracted capsule.

The voice of a Grey Treefrog resonates from above on a tree trunk, a high pitched bleating, and I realize that we have been hearing Spring Peepers too, just a few peeps at intervals, their autumn song. I breathe the fresh perfume of wet fallen leaves and wet bark. A wave of autumn migrant birds suddenly surrounds me with sharp squeaks, but I can see none. Jennie saw one baby Wood Frog but failed to catch it.

Fred shouted "*Dirca palustris*" and beckoned me over to admire Leatherwood, a widely branching bronze-barked bush. Its branches resist breaking, almost as supple as leather. Its bark has been used as bowstring. Its smooth sinuousness reminds me of *Arbutus* trees of the West Coast, but it grows no more than head-high. I see a round snail sleeping on a branch of this bush about a metre above ground. A beetle falls from my hat brim, brushed by my hand – a short-faced little weevil that must have come onto my hat from the Leatherwood leaves. I let it walk on my page as I write notes. It is a pale ivory tan, almost pinkish, with short bars of brown up its sides, black eyes, black mouth parts, and rather long, elbowed antennae. The snail awakens and begins to creep up the Leatherwood branch. I collect it to draw.

Fred and Jennie turned rocks in a

sandy spring stream. Jennie saw a frog which proved to be a Pickerel Frog, the common spotted frog of the Maritimes and New England, but this is only the fourth place we've ever found them in Ontario. At the foot of a short slope of mud and mossy stones, the spring wells up from sand, keeping the fine grains dancing in a pool no larger than a cereal bowl. From there a little stream trickles away around softly moss-pelted stones on a sandy bed about a metre and a half wide. The trail bends away from it to the left between bunches of crisp dark Christmas Fern, a few knee-high bushes of Leatherwood, and drooping yellow False Solomon's Seal, red berries gone from their shrivelled twiggy tips. We've turned back from dark Hemlock shade into the busy, leafy green light of young Maples. Horsetails poke like forest of tall green drinking straws from the leaf litter amidst a sea of jagged little maple leaves. Jack-in-the-Pulpit raises bunches of startling red berries on short single stalks, with two damp tissue thin rags of its leaves flopped out on either side. We've returned to the dry creek bed, upstream of the first bridge, and climb up the slope past

Plethodon cinereus

young Ironwoods, to Birches at the top, past a giant White Pine and back past the first bridge.

RAFTON CREEK, Haldimand, 29 September

Early on the evening of 19 September the harvest moon rose full and orange, pumpkin-like above Lakeshore Road. We follow the moon later as it moves toward the lake, rising and paling from a golden coin to a silver quarter high above the beach. Certain of the incoming waves glisten like living white fire, and the regular rhythm of their breaking roar is like the breathing of a great sleeping beast. Fred pauses to pick up a Toad who has come down to wet its skin in the lake, and I cross the creek on the firm sand bar that the boisterous surf of earlier in the day has cast across its mouth.

I set up my stool to draw the creek mouth and lake waves in the moonlight. Jennie is building an elaborate fireplace to make a fire and keep me company, but the cool damp breeze at my back slips its fingers inside my collar, and I'm tired and need to go to bed, so drawing the moonlit scene in my mind, we walk back to camp.

After a few nights of thunderstorm and days of cloud and rain, I return to the creek mouth to get a

Rana palustris

134

real-place reference for the full moon scene as I remember it, to decorate my capital G. The sky is breaking into fits of sunshine, and the lake is wrathful, stirring itself into a peevish green-grey. The waves rear and curl and fall solidly, three or four rows of them at once, beginning far out from shore.

The water of the creek pools slightly before spilling in riffles out over the breast of sand to the waves. The creek mouth has a cobbly bank, but its bottom is a soft sandy bed patched with rich green pipecleaner forests of Pondweed. A little bridge supported by a double arch of wooden roof trusses spans the creek a stone's throw from the beach.

Just beyond the bridge, a steep-banked pond is being dug, over the course of three winters, to increase wetland diversity by suppressing Purple Loosestrife. Now a modest scattering of that species shares the sandy banks with Cattails, Burr Reed, large round-stemmed *Scirpus*, heavy-podded clumps of Iris and others. Purple Loosestrife, *Lythrum salicaria*, is no relation to the yellow-flowered Loosestrifes, which are primroses. Introduced long ago from Europe, at least in part as a garden plant, it has been increasingly noticed as a menace in the past 20 years, dominating wet habitats as diverse as the low spots in Corn fields and orchid bogs. In a corner of this site that has not yet been dug up, we can see that it reduced the vegetation to a tall stand of itself over a soil cover of moss. Exotic species are usually most invasive when they first

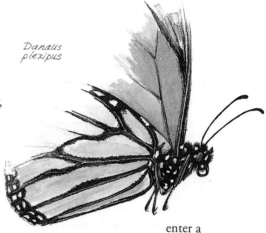

Danaus plexipus

enter a region, so one wonders why Purple Loosestrife has spread recently. Perhaps it has evolved adaptations to local conditions faster than herbivores have adapted to it; perhaps changed patterns of land use have expanded its habitat; or perhaps general environmental degradation, increased ultraviolet light or acid rain, or toxic deposition has favoured this hardy species.

Here the tenacious purple has been replaced by a bold display of opportunistic glory, a solid yellow band of *Bidens* 1-3 m wide all around the western side of the pond. To the dismay of the careful owner of Collie Dogs, every brown eye of the cheerful golden mass of daisy-like flowers is maturing an arsenal of flat brown seeds

Thimbleberry Rubus odoratus

135

with two clinging teeth each: "Bi-dens" means two-teeth. At this stage of the succession of this wetland, *Bidens* has found a place along the lip of the pond, dominating temporarily until other plants push in.

The wavy-edged pond, dug with islands and bays, is flanked by two shallow settling or filtering ponds. The one on the west, just behind the beach, is bristling with a healthy bed of Burr Reed. The eastern settling pond is open and shallow, beginning to grow patches of pond lilies, Frogbit, Cattail, Burr Reed, and other emergent and also submergent plants. Black-bodied Ramshorn snails graze on the pale bottom near the western edge, and dragonfly nymphs, camouflaged with silt, hunt in water warmed by the sun.

Under tall Black Cherry trees on the eastern side, a walking path has been mowed through thick stands of Goldenrod and Asters, Dogwood, Chokecherry and Thimbleberry. Tall whorls of Ostrich Fern, which in summer are giant feathery vases, now stand tired and brown-speckled about their neat centres of short, dark fertile fronds. Tall Blackberry canes are withered and leafless, the last of their dark glossy fruit now small and shrivelled. The last pink flower of Thimbleberry is crumpled from the heavy rains. But still there are sweet, tender red fruits to pull carefully – fleshy thimbles – from the large white cones of their receptacles. The intense flavour and rich texture of Thimbleberries make them rather like fresh jam that never needs cooking – just picking!

At the upper end of the pond, a Cedar pole bridge takes the path across the creek above a little waterfall, to follow the bank toward the lake, and then into a grove of White Cedar, where a network of paths fans out to various house lots. Back across the pole bridge, I returned to Nawautin Road, through light woods of tall Birches, Aspens and scattered Cedars, with an open understorey of Elderberry drooping flat clusters of glossy black berries. The ground cover is Sensitive Fern, its broad, simple fronds yellowing, as its name indicates, from sensitivity to the first frosts of autumn. I came out to the road past *Smilax* vines, with their tightly packed globes of blue berries held out on ridiculously long stems. A tall Highbush Cranberry stands at the end of the path, not a true Cranberry, but a *Viburnum*, drooping sour clusters of large, violently vermillion berries. These can be cooked and used like Cranberries, and are best after autumn frosts have made their flesh transparent.

ONARCHS are still moving through. I have held and painted one with a broken wing. It sits on Jennie's hand in the trailer and sips honey and water. Jennie feeds the wasps too, but we persuaded her to take the feeding station out of the trailer. Though they have been tolerant of our movements at close quarters, we don't want to sit on one by accident, or find any in our bedding in the dark. We suppose these are native Yellowjackets. The European "Picnic Wasps,"

Vespula germanica, are much more inclined to sting. In the evenings, young Cottontails sit on our grassy path and, later, Coyotes howl in keening, yammering chorus.

Grafton Creek to Colborne, Haldimand & Cramahe, 29 September

The afternoon was overcast, windy and cool as Fred biked towards Colborne following the Waterfront Trail along Lakeshore Road. Rain threatened from fast-moving clouds as he passed second-growth habitats, Poplar, Maple and Cedar woods, old fields growing up in Aspen and Cedar, a lakeshore trailer park and a swampy forest of mixed woods, meeting remnants of Toad, Meadow Vole and Garter Snake on the road. In the fall when amphibians move on rainy nights and reptiles migrate on occasional warm days, our survey of their distribution relies on cars and trucks to intercept unfortunate wanderers. Then we bicycle past later, identifying their remains. By recording the existence of their species and relative numbers at that place, we diminish the waste of their death.

At the new Wicklow Beach boat launch a heavy surf on the gravel beach of flattened pebbles has driven a new drift of sticks, feathers, and rootstocks and stems of water plants up almost to the level of the old drift we met there this spring.

The road heads straight east toward Lakeport, leaving the shoreline as much as half a kilometre to the south, past Apple orchards, second-growth woods, hayfields, pastures and scattered roadside houses. The air was calm about Fred while he pedalled, but he was discouraged from stopping by the stiff west wind that whipped about him whenever he paused to write notes or identify Leopard and Green Frog scraps on the road. He continued along Lakeshore Road, passing Ontario Street where the Waterfront trail route loops down through Lakeport, an open grassy settlement behind a narrow gravel beach with picturesque old Willows. During our auditory survey this spring we heard Toads, Peepers and Grey Treefrogs in a swamp of Black Willows where Colborne Creek flows past the end of Mill Street, but the Peepers only came there after their breeding chorus had ended somewhere to the northwest. Perhaps the absence of Peeper breeding in creek-mouth swamps has more to do with lake fluctuations or predators in the lake than disturbance by people.

It was too windy to find anything in the marsh of Narrow-leaved Cattail west of town, so he met us back in Lakeport.

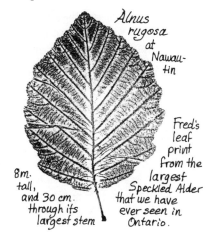

Alnus rugosa at Nawau-tin

8m. tall, and 30 cm. through its largest stem

Fred's leaf print from the largest Speckled Alder that we have ever seen in Ontario.

12

Presqu'ile Camp

We left Grafton at noon of 3 October, and have moved into site 106 in the public campground in Presqu'ile Provincial Park, a lakeside Red Pine plantation on sand, and were greeted by calls of Peepers and Wood Frogs. Elderberry bushes make up the understorey, and Garlic Mustard blankets the ground. The crowns of the Pines above our trailer are alive with the movements of birds, picking, cleaning, grooming the trees, as they fatten for the night and the winter: Blackcap Chickadees, Whitebreast Nuthatch, Downy Woodpecker and Brown Creeper.

Colborne, 4 October

Today we shuttle back to Colborne, to pick up the thread of our explorations and continue it eastward.

Wrapped in coats and sleeping bags, my big umbrella set up against the cold wind, I sit on a folding stool in the village green of the little town of

Colborne on 4 October, when we should have been home a month ago. At the other end of the grassy park from where I sit drawing, Jennie plays with local children on slides and ladders. Behind me, two cannon from 1844 hold ground at the south end of the park, and an eroding limestone statue of a soldier of the Great War stands guard. In the centre of my sketch, a granite memorial to World War II is planted about with tiny-bloom Begonias and a frosty-leaved ground cover. Nearby, an oversize red plastic Apple with a white valentine heart on it perches on a green concrete tripod pedestal.

Shop fronts peek out behind and under the park trees, and people walk across the park on their way to anywhere, which seems to slow the pace of the town. I'm charmed by the way in which the park is the very centre of town, and completely surrounded by it, an unusual pattern in Ontario, as most Loyalist settlements abandoned the commons-centred plan of the New England towns they'd left.

While I worked at my drawing Fred checked Colborne Creek and found two adult *Cambarus*

138

limestone quarry

bartoni crayfish, and the shadowy shapes of big fish in the shelter of the culvert. In the late afternoon, he headed eastward on Hwy 2 and south on Durham Street to a beach access and the cottage row of Victoria Beach. The long peninsula of Presqu'ile was visible to the east and the sunset sky displayed all types of clouds, from cumulus to stratus to cirrus. Two Common Loons loafed among mixed gulls and a flock of a hundred Mergansers flew low over the lake on white-patched wings. A little farther along the shore, a sand beach turned to one of "skipping stones," and looking to the east, Fred could see the long conveyor belt of the cement quarry.

He returned to meet us in Colborne just as I was finishing my sketch, stiff and chilled and ready for my thermos of hot tea.

Colborne to Presqu'ile, 5 October

At Victoria Beach we enter the gate of the St. Lawrence Cement Company. Past a stretch of wild Cedar and Hemlock woods our view opens suddenly across a huge quarry like a dry lake bottom to the far distant shore, an escarpment of evenly bedded limestone. Distant monster dumptrucks bring loads of blasted stone across the wide plain of the quarry bottom, to tip down into the workings of a conveyor. The road runs past a mountainous pile spanned by the straight, narrow bridge of the conveyor track and looking up, we watch crushed limestone fall like garden soil onto the top of the pile. Another conveyor track emerges like an uphill rollercoaster from the bottom of the pile toward the loading dock that runs out into the lake off Ogden Point. Here it is loaded into ships and carried to the manufacturing plant we passed in Mississauga. As Fred and

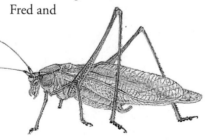

Katydid

139

Jennie prepare their bicycles for the run east to Presqu'ile, I go into the low office to get permission to park by the quarry to paint. The quarry boss came by at closing time and looking at my work, said he supposed there must be beauty in everything.

When I caught up with Fred and Jennie, I learned that after finding a road-killed Garter Snake at the gate, they had cycled past fields and bluff-edge houses along Victoria Beach. They passed a Christmas tree farm, roadside Apple trees and wild Grape in fruit. Jennie found a shiny live *Cochlicopa* snail in the blossom end of a fallen Apple, and they saw a Harrier over a lakeside field. A little farther east, discovering fruiting clumps of Wild Raisins, they sucked the flat pits out of the dark, pasty cinnamon-sweet berries and continued on to Blyth Park Road, which ends at a 4-m bluff and a beach of coarse gravel. Here they walked a little way along the beach, but found no invertebrates in the drift of rolled *Chara*, just a line of Bank Swallow nest holes in the sandy layer at the top of the bluff.

After it drops its leaves in the autumn,

Witch Hazel blooms.

North along Simpson Drive to Salem Creek, they passed Bittersweet, *Celastrus*, in sheathed berry, draped over roadside fences, and many Black Locust trees. Salem Creek runs wide, clear and rocky through a Horse pasture and an old field. The scene was ennobled by "Keep Out" signs on the creek, and the fences of the pastures were wired directly to the metal of the culvert so the road allowance stretch of the stream was not available for sampling.

Where the road turned north, they followed the CN tracks to a Cedar-surrounded wetland of Broadleaf Cattail, grass and sedge, where they caught a katydid, conspicuously green between the ties of the tracks, and brought it back for me to paint. A sand and peat-bottomed creek drains the wetland under the railway, and dense stiff stands of Horsetail dominate the top of the slag and cinder embankment.

At Bellamy Road Fred and Jennie found wetlands on all four sides of the intersection between road and tracks: drawn-down Beaver ponds, Cattail marsh, yellowish purple down-bent stems of a *Decodon* swamp, and swampy woods. They returned to Hwy 2 on the next cross-road, finding a Witch Hazel bush on the sandy roadside, blooming as they do in the autumn. They brought back a twig of its touselled spidery flowers with string-like yellow petals.

For a short stretch on Hwy 2, Fred and Jennie were the first bicyclists to use the new black-paved shoulders of this segment of the Waterfront Trail, and then they went south on Barnes Road and stood on a high bridge over the CN tracks, above brushy old fields and Aspen second growth. I saw them there, but squinting into the bright sunset, they didn't see me. As they continued south past swamps to the lakeshore, I caught up with them, I caught up on them, and then went on ahead to Unnamed Wetland #2 to begin the drawing for my painting. They found me parked beside my grassy creek-mouth marsh, separated from the lake by a long Willow-lined bar. My eyes and brush explored its narrow borders of Cattails, floating lily pads and bushy islands of Dogwood and Willows, and I hope to someday launch a canoe and discover it at close hand.

Jennie stayed with me in the truck as I drew the scene, and Fred went east, pushing on through the falling dusk past old fields being encroached on and crowded out by houses, almost like the flow of a viscous fluid. Light was failing when he reached Popham Bay at the end of Huff Road. He took quick note of a wide-lawn subdivision there, with a coarse gravel beach and a view of the long black shape of Presqu'ile, and he reached camp at 19:20 in the dark.

Presqu'ile Park, Brighton, 6 October
While Fred bicycled to Trenton, Jennie and I set out to cruise Presqu'ile. Just east of Owen Point, the elbow of the peninsula, we find a steep coarse gravel beach strewn with feathers, bones and carcases of juvenile Ringbill Gulls,

washed from breeding colonies on islands offshore. There is an autumnal chill in the westerly breeze, and the lake is grey and opaque. Offshore two islands are grey against the sultry pink sky. High Bluff is the farthest one, and to the west of it lies Gull Island, so low that it is only a charcoal line on the water, with a few bare-branched bushes scribbled up from it.

A small marsh cut off from the lake by the shore road is ringed by the arched stems of *Decodon*, untidily crested with reddening foliage, and two families of Mallards explode into quacks, splashes and whirring wings as we pass. Returning through our own campground, we head out into the maze of park roads. We drive north first, through a tall forest of mixed deciduous trees, with a thick undergrowth of ferns, Raspberry and Jewelweed, and then through alternating waves of Pine and deciduous woods. Then we turn east through a forest of Mature Sugar Maples, where the Horsetail *Equisetum hyemale* grows dull and dark in deep green shade, like grass under the trees. Then the road leads through mixed woods again and out

Goldenrod & Buckthorn

141

"Un-named
Wetland #2"
4 Km. E.S.E.
Salem, Ontario

into the open of a lawn-park picnic ground above a steep narrow beach and the wide green lake, where Crows walk on the clipped grass. A smooth paved road takes us east through Maple, Cedar and Spruce forest, shady and ferny and inviting closer investigation, but it's 18:00 and our rendezvous with Fred in Trenton is pressing, so we pause to jot quick notes then roll on along the smooth forest road, past a quaint gift shop, to the tip of the peninsula, where a wooden lighthouse stands before the bay and the distant curve of Prince Edward County. The light dims toward dusk as we take the road westward along the north side, watching for deer eating Apples in the old orchards.

Presqu'ile to Trenton, 6 October

On a calm, cool and sunny afternoon, Fred set off from camp toward Trenton, treating himself to a "binge of biodiversity, as plants and animals finally reach the kind of variety we would expect along Hwy 7 or at home." He left the park along a gravel path that runs along south of Harbour Street to our auditory station at the boat-launch west of Gosport.

At the water's edge a small stand of Flowering Rush bears umbels of rounded matte-black seeds. On the rough gravel embankment, he found one nearly intact Snapping Turtle egg among the shells around 10 rifled turtle nests. Four Leopard Frogs sat on the bank near the culvert. A single bout of calling here on the night of 29 May is our westernmost record of a Bull Frog, and it was nicely confirmed by a large male basking at the water's edge.

He found Harbour Park tucked in among the lakeside cottages and boathouses on a richly vegetated clearwater shore. The bank was a tangle of *Bidens*, Pink Jewelweed, Purple Loosestrife, Cattails and Cocklebur along a shore of coarse gravel and flat stones. The submerged Duckweed *Lemna trisulca* made up most of the voluminous drift

Wild Raisin
Viburnum
Lentago.

and
formed
green clouds in
the weedy clear
water just off-
shore, where the
eelgrass Wild
Celery was the
dominant rooted plant, with corkscrew
reproductive stems and sausage-like
fruits. The bottom was littered with the
very old chalky shells of Horn Snails,
and turning rocks revealed a few
Orconectes propinquus, a large freshly
dead shell of *Anodonta grandis* and a
fragment of *Lasmigona compressa*, the
first time we have found two species of
unionid mussel together.

Moving into Gosport, past rows of
little houses into an area of marinas
and newer houses with Florida-like canal access to the water, he came to the
Cedar Street Picnic Area, a little fill-
built promontory labelled "Town of
Brighton Observation Point." There
were lots of vascular water weeds offshore, but the bottom quickly dropped
off to a navigable depth. Green Frog
tadpoles wriggled out of his way, big
mottled greenish *Orconectes propinquus*
lurked under stones, and he briefly saw
the wide flat pale-sided head of a large
adult Mudpuppy, but it retired and the
water was so easily muddied that he
was not able to see it again. People are

always impressed when they see a
Mudpuppy, the largest of Canadian
salamanders, with its orange
tail fin and its external
gills like red ostrich
plumes.

Where Har-
bour Street runs
between Brighton
and Gosport, Fred
stopped at the little water-
management structure at
Procters Creek, reminiscent
of those at Shoreacres and
Appleby creeks. This clear cold
40-cm-deep Watercress stream,
running past houses, Manitoba Maples
and Willows, had abundant *Orconectes
propinquus* under concrete slabs below
the bridge, and Dace under the stones
dashing frantically around when un-
covered.

Then he rolled up to County Road
64 and to our auditory station 1 km
north of Gosport, between a sewage lagoon and lakeshore Cattail marshes. At
the gate he found a very flat, dry juvenile Leopard Frog, the first
herpetological roadkill of an afternoon
when roadkills went from the Toronto-
like paucity that has prevailed west of
here to the abundant signature of large
populations that we are familiar with at
home and on the Bruce Peninsula.

What follows is a travelogue of
roadkills, a still-life, as it were, arranged
by automobile transportation. Fred
found a cross-section, some percentage
of the life that had crossed the roads,
though travelling at bicycle speed, he
missed many insects. Although it is sad

to see life wasted, he rejoiced to finally find a world with enough life to make that cross-section visible. The popular opinon of roadkills has been influenced by the sight of large mammals crushed by multiple impacts. Most People never see most roadkills. I've often stopped everything to stay and paint a bird. Most small roadkills that haven't been thoroughly flattened and sun-dried to a crisp, are picked up by Crows or Vultures, scavenged at night by Skunks or Raccoons, or dragged off and buried by big back-and-orange Silphid beetles.

County Road 64 runs across a gentle agricultural slope north of Presqu'ile Bay, past cattle feedlots, a road-killed adult Ringbill Gull and a Raccoon, past fallow and Corn fields, and road-killed young Milk Snake, Leopard Frogs, Redbelly Snake, Mourning Dove, juvenile Garter Snake and a Meadow Vole. Rolling into the settlement called Lovett on the map and Murray Canal on the road sign, Fred crossed the bridge over the canal, finding remain of Bull Frog and Garter Snake. He continued east along County Road 64, south of the canal, past houses, woods and Strawberry fields, recording countless frog remnants, five Garter Snakes, three Snapping Turtle hatchlings, an adult Painted Turtle and a fresh Meadow Vole.

North on the gravel road to the south bank of the Murray Canal, toads joined the list of road-killed species, and near the canal bank there were juvenile Water Snakes as well. This road comes out just across from our Murray Canal auditory station, and Fred turned east on the narrow gravel road that hugs the canal's south bank.

The Murray Canal runs straight as a ruler on the map, 7 km from Presqu'ile Bay to the Bay of Quinte. Its steep banks are armoured by rock rubble except at the masonry of the few bridges. The little-used gravel road along the south bank runs on the top of the embankment between the canal and a large Cattail marsh. At the bridge over the slow outlet stream from the marsh, a Snipe and a pair of Black Ducks flew up, and a Bull Frog waited in the water. Under the rocks in the outlet, which were gritty with minute Zebra Mussels, he found two *Orconectes propinquus*.

Meeting a live adult Leopard Frog on the bank was a pleasant change after the mortality on faster roads. A black Squirrel ran towards Fred along the embankment east of the outlet, and turned aside into a thicket of Wild Raisin and Apple. Along the rest of the canal to Hwy 33, 10 more Leopard Frogs, and *Sorex* and a Shorttail Shrew joined the account of the slain. He crossed a bridge and went north on Hwy 33. Cycling along in evening light on a newly paved highway shoulder, he passed the cattail marshes at the head of Dead Creek, and enjoying low-lying vistas past pastures and farmhouses to the Bay of Quinte. He threaded his way along residential streets and finally up onto the bridge over the Trent River. High on the new-concrete bridge over the placid water of the canal-river, he looked south to the Bay of Quinte and across the towers of Trenton into a pale beige sunset.

Heading down into the dark of east Trenton, he tried to reach W. Bains Park by the Municipal Trail shown, perhaps prematurely, on the Waterfront Trail map, but it led him into dead end parking lots. I had similar experiences in the truck, and both of us had to go north to Hwy 2 to rendezvous at the park where we had seen Map Turtles in June. There may be a trail along the shore, but we cannot find it in the dark. We eat soup that I had brought in a thermos, and try to phone home to report our arrival at the eastern end of the Waterfront Trail, but Fred's Mother isn't at her phone, so we load up, pry Jennie off the swings, and drive back to camp.

Presqu'ile Park, beaches & dunes north of Owen Point, 7 October

Back at camp to finish our exploration of Presqu'ile, Fred did some beach walking this sunny afternoon. Fred went farther out on the sandspit of Owen Point than Jenny and I had and turned up many more unionid mussels than we have found west of here. He found a Leopard Frog active among the upper beach herbs and another under a piece of plywood, and saw Deer and Raccoon tracks in the mud.

The sunlight was blinding over the wide flats of algal felt north of the point, where a few shorebirds wandered. There were many snails on the surface of the algae, juvenile carapaces and larger chelipeds of the crayfish *Orconectes propinquus*, and the battered wings of Monarch Butterflies. Quick identification by Wayne Grimm of the bagful of shells Fred picked up reveals 25 species of small molluscs, of which four are European introductions: *Bithynia tentaculata* (European Faucet snail), *Dressensia polymorpha* (Zebra Mussel), *Radix auricularia* (European Ear Snail), and *Valvata piscinalis* (European Valve Snail). Twelve are native snails: *Gyraulus circumstriatus* (Flatly Coiled Gyraulus), *Gyraulus deflectus*, *Helisoma anceps* (Two-ridged Ramshorn), *Physa gyrina* (Tadpole Snail), *Physa sayi*, *Pleurocera acuta*, *Probythinella lacustris*, *Stagnicola catascopium* (Lake Stagnicola), *Valvata perdepressa*, *Valvata sincera helicoidea* and *Valvata tricarinata* (Three-keeled Valve Snail), and nine are Sphaerid Clams: *Pisidium cf castertanum* (Ubiquitous Pea Clam), *Pisidium compressum* (Ridged-Beak Pea Clam), *Pisidium virginianum*, *Pisidium amnicum*, *Sphaerium fabale*, *Sphaerium lacustre*, *Sphaerium securis* (Pond Fingernail Clam), *Sphaerium striatinum* (Striated Fingernail Clam) and *Sphaerium transversa*. There are shells of four Unionid mussels, *Anodonta grandis simpsoniana*, *Anodontoides ferrussacianus*, *Lampsilis radiata siliquoidea* and *Strophitus undulatus*.

As Fred worked along the beach, I took Jennie, her campground friend and Bear for a visit to the dunes at the neck of the Presqu'ile Peninsula, where the marsh is closest to the lake. The beach parking lot is among low dunes, in a parkland of stunted, ridge-barked Cottonwoods. As we walk out beneath them to the road, their gold-coin leaves flutter against the blue late-afternoon sky.

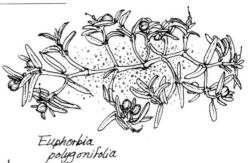

Euphorbia polygonifolia

We come through a field of Dogwood and White Cedar, then cross the park road to a dry flat of fen-looking vegetation, dominated by the yellowing narrow-leaved Twig-Rush. Purple Loosestrife was purple-leaved with dry brown flower spikes. Tiny white *Aster* flowers sparkled in the dry rough turf and ferny Silverweed patterned the ground like a mediaeval tapestry. Narrow-spired groups of the juniper, Eastern Red Cedar stand 4 m tall. Green and blue berries pearl their tight braids of resinous foliage. In the lowest places the Twig-Rush turf opens up into low mossy patches, now cracked and dry, where Variegated Horsetail, banded with white and black nodes, forms a bristly turf.

At the foot of the dune grow clumps of ferny, aromatic *Artemesia*, in open sand marked by tracks of mice and shrews, and Crows dragging their hind claws. As we start up the dry sand slope of the high dunes, I notice a round hole in the sand, a wasp burrow. About the size of my baby finger, it is haloed by 3 or 4 cm of

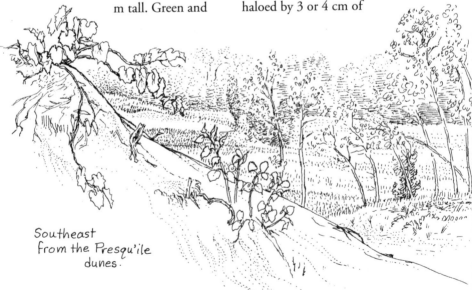

Southeast from the Presqu'ile dunes.

thrown-out sand and rimmed with a stand-up collar, a delicate sandy membrane still moist from the wasp's attentions. The whole thing is obliterated by Bear, before I can show it to the girls. We find two hard white shells of *Anguispira alternata*, one with still a trace of its checked pattern. How land snails can have come to such a dry sandy place is a mystery.

Halfway up the dune I draw the little dune specialist, *Euphorbia polygonifolia*, where it embroiders itself into the sand with pink succulent roots and branches, little folded leaves and round green fruit pods. We climb to the top of the dune, and on the crest find white shards of torn Snapping Turtle eggs, scattered about the predator-opened nest among short Grape vines with toothy yellow leaves. Poison Ivy grows here too, its leaflets autumn-orange and waxy in this exposed habitat. Here is also a short-stemmed lily with dark ruby berries and lax dead leaves, *Maianthemum stellatum*.

Over the Cedar-hedged crest, we descended abruptly to the marsh at the foot of the shaded east side of the dunes, brushing through Dogwood bushes, Goldenrod, and the nodding wheat-like grass, *Elymus canadensis*. The steep sandy slope, draped with dead grey *Equisetum hyemale* Horsetail, stops abruptly at a stand of tall green grass which grades into the cattails of the marsh.

The view across the marsh is beautiful and golden far out to the blue bay and the line of trees and cottages along the shore. Beyond lie distant purple hills of autumnal forest. It's hard to resist doing a watercolour of this, but I came to draw in ink, so turn away and sit in the sand to draw the view southwest over the "dry fen" until dusk.

Presqu'ile Park, 8 October

The autumnal calling of several Wood Frogs and a rousing chorus of Peepers ended at dawn this morning, and we have a clear day to break camp and hike the marsh boardwalk before driving home.

As I pack up, Fred makes leaf prints of three remarkable exotic plants from our campsite. We have seen the round, reticulately-veined leaves of *Alliaria officinalis*, Garlic Mustard, in woods all along the lakeshore, but the single rosette of long soft ferny leaves, *Chelidonium majus*, called Swallowwort or Celandine, a poppy whose toxic yellow juice was once used medicinally, and the twining clump of *Humulus japonicus*, Japanese Hops, are both new to us.

Walking out along the long loop of the Presqu'ile Park Marsh Boardwalk, we find a sunny, breezy marsh dominated to an unusual extent by the narrow-headed Narrowleaved Cattail, *Typha angustifolia*. In most lakeside marshes hybrids between this species and the Broadleaved Cattail, *Typha latifolia*, make up most of the population, but here these show very little hybrid influence. *T. angustifolia* used to be considered a native species, but study of old floras has shown that through the 19th century it spread across the eastern part of North

America, just as it has continued across the prairies in this century, suggesting that it was introduced from Europe.

Several big *Lymnea stagnalis* snails, grey bodies and fragile high-spired shells, creeping on the surface of the exposed mud, are the only molluscs we see from the boardwalk. Signs on the boardwalk tell of the damage Carp do to the marsh, but we see only one Largemouth Bass. The variety of submerged plants suggests that, compared with points west of here, there are relatively few Carp in this marsh.

From an observation tower we scan the open water of the marsh with the spotting scope and see fishing Great Blue Herons, lots of Mallards and Canada Geese, many Coots, several Redheads, one Pied-bill Grebe and a drake Wood Duck. A young couple with a wet Cat on a leash come up the tower and then go back down again, having met us up here with Bear.

The path back to the parking lot takes us through the Cedar woods of one of the forested ridges that finger out into the marsh. The woods are open and roomy with

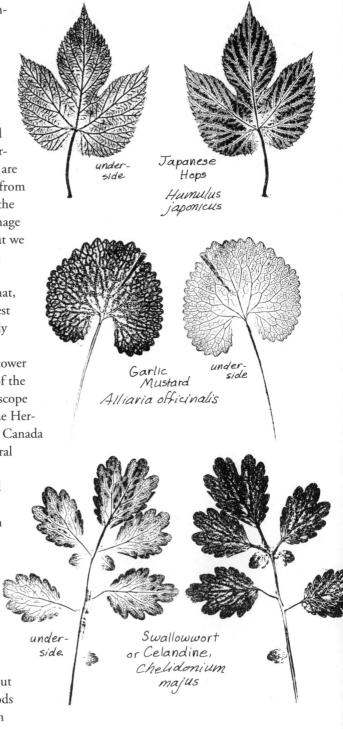

under-side

Japanese Hops
Humulus japonicus

Garlic Mustard
Alliaria officinalis

under-side

under-side

Swallowwort or Celandine,
Chelidonium majus

smooth springy leaf litter and sweeping columns of sinuous fibre-barked trunks. The bases of some of the trunks are humped and stretched taut where they were once borne down by fallen comrades. On these saddle-shaped curves, the rosy bark is silky and wrinkled finely as if stretched. Jennie mounts them like Horses, embracing their strong "necks."

A few scattered Cottonwoods stand among the Cedars, with thick corky bark and kidney-shaped leaves – pure *Populus deltoides* with no hint of hybridization with *P. balsamifera*. The picturesque bark of the trunks is deeply split, with very high relief, as if the Cedar woods protect them from the abrasion of the open air, or as if they grow here very slowly. We see a clump of Common Juniper, usually a sprawling bush, grown into a cluster of 6 m sinuous trees with splotches of white crustose lichen on their bark. This is the most tree-like Common Juniper we have ever seen; perhaps like the Cottonwoods it is protected by the dense Cedar woods.

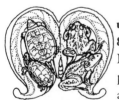 **urray Canal, 8 October** Now we are off, pulling the trailer along Fred's route of two days ago to the Murray Canal. We stop where the outflow of the Cattail marsh runs under the gravel road into the canal. The marsh spreads out like an unbroken field of hybrid Corn, all the way to the far wall of Red Maples, whose green is turning to diverse shades of crimson, vermillion, orange and purple.

In the spring we had two auditory stations on the north bank of the canal, where we heard Peepers, Chorus Frogs, Leopard Frogs, Toads, Treefrogs, Green Frogs and Bull Frogs. Now we hear a few Peepers calling and see a Garter Snake basking on a canalside rock.

We have stopped here for Wild Raisins, *Viburnum lentago*. From the tall, many-trunked bush on the marshside embankment, its smooth bare branches sweep down in an untidy tangle. The large oval leaves are mostly green yet. Long-stemmed berries, oval and black, droop from the twig ends, with some rosy-cheeked and green ones yet to ripen. They are sweet, not sour or tart, with a spicy flavour like cinnamon. Young shoots of the bush grow on the west side in the sun, spreading out along the bank just above the cattails, straight vertical whips graced with vermillion leaves that curve down like those of Wild Cherry. There are many clumps of this species along the canal, recognizable by the colour of their turned leaves, but no others in fruit. We collected two gallon-baskets of ripe berry bunches, took them home and made them into a rich sticky jam.

149

13

Living with the Lake

Before settlement, the waters of Lake Ontario were not as rich in nutrients as they are now. No great rivers brought minerals and nutrients from the land. Dissolved nutrient salts were filtered from rainwater by the rootwebs of the great forests and lost by sedimentation in deep basins. When settlement began to open up the forests, soil eroded from cultivated fields and cut-over land, unleashing a flood of nutrients, which was later increased by domestic sewage, runoff from fertilized fields, industrial organic wastes and phosphate detergents. Increased surface concentrations of phosphate, especially, led to a simplification of the complex phytoplankton, replacing silica-shelled diatoms with nitrogen-fixing blue-green cyanobacteria. The new system favours a different community of animal plankton, which in turn favours Alewives at the expense of native whitefish.

Although toxins that accumulate in animals are invisible, the persistence of Mirex and PCBs in Lake Ontario is notorious, and deformed birds, frogs and crayfish remind us that such pathologies do result from man-made poisons in land, air and water. Eating one predatory fish provides more toxins than a lifetime of drinking lake water. The official restrictions on eating fish from Lake Ontario are less strin-gent than they were 20 years ago, but still restrict such fish to a dietary frill. Many predatory birds and mammals can eat nothing else.

The settling of particles from effluents, leakage, fallout and contaminated fill has continued for decades and there is vastly more toxic material in bottom sediments than in the water itself, and lake-fill parks block currents that would carry sediments to burial in deep water. When the bottoms of bays or harbours are disturbed by dredging or changed currents, these toxins can enter the water and food chain. Because water takes centuries to flow through all the Great Lakes, changes in water quality have consequences that last much longer than they would in streams.

We saw both fading and invading species among mollusc shells drifted on the shore, but there is a long litany of failed and invading species in every taxon. Among predatory fish, Atlantic Salmon, Lake Char, Burbot and Blue Walleye are gone, and among plankton-eaters four Ciscos disappeared in order of decreasing size, and were followed by Lake Herring and Lake Whitefish. Lake Sturgeon were uncommon by 1900, and the Deepwater Sculpin disappeared between 1953 and 1964. Among invaders, Sea Lampreys were first seen before 1850, followed by Alewives, Gizzard Shad, Smelt and White Perch. Rainbow Trout, Brown Trout, Carp and Goldfish were introduced about a century ago. Plantings of Pacific salmon, *Oncorhynchus*, began in 1873, but only since the late 1960s have they become abundant. Rudd, a foot-long European minnow, has appeared recently, and other fish from ships' ballast water, now established in other Great Lakes, will eventually reach Lake Ontario.

People also have direct effects on animal populations. Birds and mammals have become much more trusting since People stopped shooting at them, but the great numbers killed on roads doubtless keep many amphibian, reptile and mammal populations small.

Many of the urban stretches of the Waterfront shoreline and stream corridors have become public reserves, though these are often maintained as not-very-natural habitats. Shores of parkland are often steepened and hardened, and lake-fill parks continue these steep shores instead of creating the shallow basins and wetlands that could help compensate for drainage and filling. Water edge lands should naturally be the ecologically most diverse habitats in the landscape, providing corridors of movement between woodlands and wetlands, and trapping plant nutrients and sediment before they reach the water as pollutants. The sensitive habitats along the Niagara Escarpment at the western end of the Waterfront are as well protected as any large feature in Ontario, though naturalists

must constantly struggle to preserve its status. The Lake Ontario Waterfront will require the same vigilance if it is to be transformed, as the WRT motto states, to "clean, green, connected, open, accessible, usable, diverse, affordable and attractive."

In a wild drainage basin, plant communities are sufficiently complete and complex that more of the major plant nutrients (fixed nitrogen, phosphorus, potassium) falls in precipitation and dust than leaves it in stream flow. Compared with this, the nutrient flows in the Waterfront seem heroically unnatural. Most nutrients are imported into the area as human foodstuffs and are exported into the lake as sewage. No streams are grossly polluted now, except for periodic flushes from storm sewers and overflows of combined sewers. Here and there huge tanks are being built to buffer those flows. Wide areas of bare ground promote erosion, and lawns and other simplified plant communities cannot effect a net extraction of nutrients from precipitation. Infiltration of water into the soil, which leads to spring-fed stream flow, is greatly reduced by the extent of pavement and by incredible bylaws that route the runoff from roofs into sewers rather than into the ground.

As natural areas become isolated by disturbed habitats, they lose species, both because of extinctions and because of the increased distances to similar natural habitats from which colonists might come. Individual populations can become extinct through ecological interactions so complex as to be accidental, so populations must be connected in a network if they are to persist. We saw many forests reduced to isolated and trampled woodlots. Marshes are similarly isolated along the shore. The Leslie Street Spit lacks species it could otherwise support because colonists can't get across the looming city. The Waterfront now has very few wetlands all the way east to Presqu'ile because People have settled on all the lower ground – Hamilton, Port Credit, Toronto, Oshawa – and filled in the big wetlands, leaving the intervening higher shores looking as if they represent the natural state of the entire Waterfront.

Allowing significant patches of mature habitats would restrict the scale of human disturbance of the landscape and ensure that every settlement will include a variety of frequently disturbed and old-growth habitats. Both agriculture and residences now occupy large areas in which natural remnants or reserves scarcely suffice for recreation and water filtration, let alone support a life of their own.

People's use of the Waterfront has changed significantly in the past century. There are too many People for the lake to support any of them: no commercial fisheries, no mining except the Colborne cement quarry, less and less shipping in the Port of Toronto. Individuals are no longer tied to the lake for their material livelihood, except to service the recreation of others. This contributes to the alienation of People from the land they live on, and the loss of their sense of place.

The Waterfront in its present state is more vital and rewarding as a subject of study than anything to be found in books or on television. Despite the hard facts of toxins, imbalance and degradation, when People are out experiencing the land and water, they find profound and compelling beauty in the life that is there. We can step out of our human self-involvement into the larger world, and with nature reclaim it together. Anyone who lives within reach of the Waterfront can devote themselves to it. Develop your sense of place as you walk, bicycle, paddle, swim, draw, paint, write, study, collect, analyse, understand and communicate. There is much that is yet unknown, and anyone who undertakes observing, recording and understanding the life of a particular life or taxon will find out new things. The less well known your subject is, the greater will be your discoveries. This young lake has been abruptly and irrevocably changed by commercial society, and it will be a sign of hope if commercial People can come to live sustainably along its shores.

APPENDIX

Anuran Auditory Stations

Since local naturalists can visit our auditory stations more frequently than we will be able to, we ask anyone who knows the calls of Ontario anurans well to listen at our stations on any night during the season, to try to hear as many species as possible. In this list the stations are located by their 1:50 000 National Topographical Map number and Universal Transverse Mercator Military Grid coordinates (explained on the topo maps). Record the time you listened, air temperature, wind and precipitation, sources of distracting noise, and species that were calling (or that none were heard), and send your records to us (RR #2 Oxford Station, Ontario K0G 1T0) or to the Ontario Herpetofaunal Summary (in care of NHIC, Box 7000, Peterborough, Ontario K9J 8M5).

In our records we record all anurans, birds and mammals that we hear and all amphibians and reptiles we see while we are listening. Intensity of calling is indicated by the Wisconsin calling index (Index One = Individuals can be counted; no overlapping of calls. Index Two = Calls of individuals are distinguished, but some calls overlap. Index Three = Full chorus; continuous calls) or by counts of individuals. We listen at a station until we are satisfied that we have heard all calling anuran species, usually 2-5 minutes, but sometimes as long as 10 minutes if there is a lot of noise. We record starting and finishing times of the visit; air temperature and wind, sky and distracting noise are described at each stop.

Long Point Bird Observatory is releasing a kit, including a call-identification tape, for volunteer monitors of amphibians in Great Lakes marshes.

MILLGROVE: Halton Co: Flamborough: 3 km W Mill Grove, large excavated yellow-water ponds, Willow brush-swamp, listen at bridge over stream. 17TNT 816 978 30M/5.

DESJARDINS CANAL: Halton Co: Dundas: Desjardins Canal/York Road, canal, Cattail marsh, Willow swamp, industrial land, listen from SE of the canal. 17TNT 863 909 30M/5.

RBG2: Halton Co: Burlington: Royal Botanic Gardens, Old Guelph Rd., Cattail-marshy pond in deciduous woods, Old Guelph Road, pull into RBG dump, walk down to pond. 17TNT 896 929 30M/5.

RBG1: Halton Co: Burlington: Royal Botanic Gardens, Valley Inn Road, Cattail-fringed lake bays, steep-slope deciduous forest, parking lot at head of Tollhouse Trail. 17TNT 904 935 30M/5.

BURLINGTON GOLF: Halton Co: Burlington: Burlington Golf Course, lakeside golf course in residential area, circular drive of club, take Shadeland from Hwy 2 E-bound. 17TNT 953 956 30M/5.

12 MILE LOOKOUT: Halton Co: Oakville: Bronte Creek, 1 km W mouth, bluff over wide creekmouth marsh, parkette overlooking creek. 17TPU 38 54 30M/5.

14 MILE CREEKMOUTH: Halton Co: Oakville: 14 Mile Creek, S of mouth, steep-banked creekmouth in deciduous woods, dead end of Wolfdale Rd. 17TPU 62 77 30M/5.

OAKVILLE CREEK: Halton Co: Oakville: Oakville Creek, 1 km NNW mouth, marshy creek in steep wooded urban valley, Trafalgar Rd., no place to stop, circle around block and park on Palmer Ave. 17TPU 74 115 30M/5.

RATTRAY MARSH: Peel Co: Mississauga: Rattray Marsh, lakeside Cattail marsh in mixed deciduous woods, path down from Bexhill St., listen at boardwalk. 17TPU 127 192 30M/12.

CREDIT RIVER: Peel Co: Mississauga: Credit R., 1 km W Port Credit, Cattail-marshy crk, urban residential valley, deadend street-stub. 17TPU 132 231 30M/12.

MARIE CURTIS: York Region: Etobicoke: .3 km SW mouth Etobicoke Creek, lawnpark/impounded creek forming marsh, willow swamp, SW-most parking lot in park. 17TPU 175 264 30M/12.

HUMBER POND: York Region: Etobicoke: Humber R 2 km NW mouth, lawn park, slow creek, oxbow willow pond, parking lot nr river, in Kings Mill Park. 17TPU 216 330 30M/11.

HUMBER BAY: York Region: Etobicoke: E Humber Bay Park, urban L. Ontario lakefill lawnpark, listen from ridge S of parking lot. 17TPU 229 307 30M/11.

GRENADIER POND: York Region: Toronto: N end Grenadier Pond, High Park, Cattail-patch urban pond in lawn park, street at foot of hill, W of N end of pond. 17TPU 233 336 30M/11.

LESLIE STREET: York Region: Toronto: Outer Harbour Headland, Reed/brush pond/swamp on filled land, where rails turn N away from road, listen at largest Cottonwood adjacent to fence S of Unwin St. 17TPU 351 343 30M/11.

BIRCHCLIFFE QUARRY: York Region: Scarborough: 1 km S Oakridge, isolated marsh in urban residential area, Warden, Clonmore SW from Hwy 2, parking lot at W end of quarry. 17TPU 387 386 30M/11.

BLUFFERS: York Region: Scarborough: SW end Bluffers Park, muddy lake lagoons, landfill lawn park, clay bluffs, SW-most end of parking lots. 17TPU 421 405 30M/14.

DANFORTH: York Region: Scarborough: Highland Creek, Old Kingston Rd. bridge, oxbow pond, swamp, creek, wooded urban lawn park ravine, Danforth Pk., between parking lot and a bridge. 17TPU 468 488 30M/14.

ROUGEMOUTH: York Region: Scarborough: 0.5 km W mouth Rouge R., Cattail estuary marsh in wooded residential valley, deadend road, neck between marshes. 17TPU 510 506 30M/14.

FRENCHMAN'S BAY: Durham Co: Pickering: N end Frenchman's Bay, head of lakeshore marsh, lawn park residential, parking lot of community centre, follow path down to bay. 17TPU 528 537 30M/14.

BAYLY CROSSING: Durham Co: Pickering: 1 km SE Glen Grove, brushy Aspen/Birch swamp, little open water, just E of RR tracks, listen on both sides of road. 17TPU 557 551 30M/14.

SQUIRES BEACH: Durham Co: Ajax: Squires Beach, L. Ontario estuary Cattail marsh, old fields, muddy little parking lot at last turn in kinky road. 17TPU 577 535 30M/14.

PICKERING BEACH: Durham Co: Ajax: Pickering Beach, housing subdivision, creek, old fields, lakeshore marsh, road S from Bayly just E of bridge, listen at bridge. 17TPU 615 549 30M/15.

LYNDE SHORES PARKING LOT: Durham Co: Whitby: 1.5 km NW mouth Lynde Creek, Cattail marsh, Willow-domin. marshside woods, old fields, listen from parking lot if BRIDGE station too noisy. 17TPU 634 576 30M/15.

LYNDE SHORES BRIDGE: Durham Co: Whitby: Lynde Ck/Victoria St, 2.5 km W Port Whitby, creekside Cattail marsh, Willow-domin. riverine woods, listen from E of bridge over creek. 17TPU 639 578 30M/15.

PORT WHITBY: Durham Co: Whitby: Port Whitby, lawn park, Cattail & mud harbour inlet, indust'l old fields, listen from S of bridge over creek. 17TPU 662 578 30M/15.

CORBETT CREEK: Durham Co: Whitby: Corbett Creek, 1 km NE Thickson Pt., Beaver-dammed Willow woods, creekmouth Cattail marsh, walk down from gate to creek crossing. 17TPU 692 576 30M/15.

PUMPHOUSE MARSH: Durham Co: Oshawa: Pumphouse Marsh, residential, lawn parks, lakeside Cattail marsh, listen from end of road W of marsh, or walk into marsh edge. 17TPU 735 582 30M/15.

HARMONY CREEK: Durham Co: Oshawa: Harmony Creek bridge, Second Marsh, marshy creek, Willow-tree swamp, sewage plant, listen from footbridge. 17TPU 750 607 30M/15.

TAUNTON: Durham Co: Newcastle: 2 km SSE Taunton, old gravel pit ponds, Cedar/mixed woods, listen at gap in woods where track goes over pile of soil. 17TPU 754 658 30M/15.

MCLAUGHLIN BAY: Durham Co: Oshawa: head McLauglin Bay, L. Ontario Cattail marsh, Willow woods, shrubbed old fields, end of road S from W-most GM parking lot. 17TPU 767 599 30M/15.

MAPLEGROVE: Durham Co: Newcastle: 2 km NNW Maple Grove, brushy swamp, excavated pond, residential, listen from intersection across from fenced pond. 17TPU 822 658 30M/15.

DARLINGTON CREEK: Durham Co: Newcastle: 1.5 km S Maple Grove, orchards, impounded creek pond, agricultural fields, listen from road above pond. 17TPU 832 632 30M/15.

WESTSIDE CREEK: Durham Co: Newcastle: mouth Westside Creek, lakeside Cattail marsh, brushy swamp, cottages, beach, end of road at creek. 17TPU 867 616 30M/15.

PORT DARLINGTON: Durham Co: Newcastle: 1 km NW Port Darlington, Cattail marsh, canalized creek above harbour, listen from parking lot below bridge. 17TPU 868 624 30M/15.

PORT NEWCASTLE: Durham Co: Newcastle: 1.5 km S Newcastle, Willow tree swamp, creek, Cattail marsh, agricultural fields, listen where road divrges from straight track down slope. 17TPU 939 637 30M/15.

NEWCASTLE STEP POND: Durham Co: Newcastle: Hwy 2, 2 km E Newcastle, 3 ponds in brook in farmhouse lawn, listen at gate to driveway, S side Hwy 2. 17TPU 953 659 30M/15.

NEWTONVILLE PICNIC AREA: Durham Co: Newcastle: Hwy 2, 3 km W Newtonville, Cedar/Hemlock/deciduous swampy forest, Cattail patches, listen at E end of picnic area. 17TPU 981 668 30M/15.

NEWTONVILLE SWAMP: Durham Co: Newcastle: 2 km ENE Newtonville, Red Maple swamp, listen at gate to track to E on slight rise in swamp. 17TQU 24 695 30M/16.

CNCP: Northumberland Co: Hope/Newcastle: 2 km W Wesleyville, railway crossing, Cattail marsh/mixed woods/Cedar & Populus 2nd growth, park between CN/CP tracks, site partly in Durham. 17TQU 54 663 30M/16.

WESLEYVILLE: Northumberland Co: Hope: 1 km E Wesleyville, industrial old fields, distant water treatment lagoons, at railway crossing. 17TQU 84 669 30M/16.

PORT BRITAIN: Northumberland Co: Hope: Port Britain, E side, deciduous tree swamp, lakeshore Cattail marsh, cottages, listen where road goes down slope from old RR embankment. 17TQU 116 674 30M/16.

W OF PORT HOPE: Northumberland Co: Hope: 3 km W Port Hope, Cedar/Pinus woods, dugouts, long abandoned old fields, crest of hill at N limit of conifer woods. 17TQU 138 703 30M/16.

E OF PORT HOPE: Northumberland Co: Hamilton: 3.5 km E Port Hope, agricultural fields, marshy beach pond, sand/shingle bar, pond at end of CN access road S from W of Hwy 2 RR crossing. 17TQU 205 703 30M/16.

CARR MARSH: Northumberland Co: Hamilton: Carr Marsh, 4 km W Cobourg, Ash/Willow swamp, ditches, wet fields, lakeside marsh, end of Bob Carr road at gate at CN tracks. 17TQU 232 706 30M/16.

COBOURG BROOK: Northumberland Co: Hamilton: Cobourg, 1 km SW Hwy 401 exit, urban cemetery, drained Cattail marsh mill pond, N end of cemetery overlooking pond. 17TQU 262 731 30M/16.

CLOVERDALE: Northumberland Co: Hamilton: 3 km N Cloverdale, brook in Cedar/mixed deciduous woods, residences, follow curving road N from Hwy 2, listen at intersection. 17TQU 294 740 30M/16.

KELLY CEMETERY: Northumberland Co: Haldimand/ Hamilton: Brookside, bluff overlooking Willow tree swamp, agricultural fields, end of road-stub S of Hwy 2. 17TQU 336 733 30M/16.

GRAFTON: Northumberland Co: Haldimand: 3 km SW Grafton, tallgrass marsh, shrubby margin, Cedar/deciduous woods, listen at gap in woods to wetland to N. 17TQU 368 726 30M/16.

BEACHMOUTH: Northumberland Co: Haldimand: 3 km SSE Wicklow, marshy creek impoundment behind lake beach bar, just W of new boat launch. 18TTD 625 733 30N/13.

LAKEPORT: Northumberland Co: Haldimand: Colburne Creek at Lakeport, creekside Willow tree-swamp near Lake Ontario, at E end of Mill Street. 18TTD 672 738 30N/13.

COLD CREEK: Northumberland Co: Cramahe: 2.5 km SE Tubbs Corners, shrub swamp, swampy grazed Aspen/Cedar woods, follow road to/from Colbourne over Hwy 401, listen at culvert. 18TTD 685 806 31C/4.

LITTLE LAKE: Northumberland Co: Cramahe: W shore Little Lake, steep-shored densely-cottaged kettle lake, follow Lillte L road N from Hwy 2, listen at parking area. 18TTD 733 804 31C/4.

SPENSER PT: Northumberland Co: Cramahe: 1.5 km NNW Spenser Pt, cultivated fields, brushy 2nd growth, park N of CP tracks. 18TTD 747 770 31C/4.

PRESQU'ILE ISTHMUS: Northumberland Co: Brighton: 1.5 km WSW Gosport, Lake Ontario Cattail marshes, lakeshore houses, causeway, enter by going straight at Harbour Street deadend sign. 18TTD 807 769 31C/4.

GOSPORT SEWAGE: Northumberland Co: Brighton: 1 km N Gosport, sewage lagoon, lakeshore Cattail marshes, ditches, County Road 64 at entrance road to sewage plant, no signage. 18TTD 821 788 31C/4.

MURRAY CANAL: Northumberland Co: Murray: 2.8 km WNW Lovett, canal and surrounding brushy second-growth, at intersection. 18TTD 895 803 31C/4.

TREMUR LAKE: Northumberland Co: Murray: 1 km SW Trenton Junction, Cattail marsh around small impoundment, at Orchard Lane, N shore of lake at inlet. 18TTD 905 871 31C/4.

12 OCLOCK: Northumberland Co: Murray: 1 km NW Twelve O'Clock Pt., escarpment ridge above lakeside Cattail marsh, at intersection. 18TTD 913 825 31C/4.

GLEN MILLER: Hastings Co: Sidney: 0.5 km W Glen Miller, Cattail-edged lagoon, backwater of rapid canal-river, park on river side of road across from pond. 18TTD 931 906 31C/4.

Index

A Place to Walk

Aleta Karstad is a free-lance museum-based biological illustrator and natural history artist and author. She was born in Guelph, Ontario, and lived in Wisconsin and Georgia as her father studied veterinary medicine and wildlife pathology, until he returned to Guelph as a professor. In 1972 she began work in biological illustration at the National Museum of Natural Sciences (now the Canadian Museum of Nature) after completing the Special Arts course at Central Technical School, Toronto, where she studied watercolour under Doris McCarthy.

Setting off on a field trip: Aleta Karstad with husband, Frederick W. Schueler, and daughter, Jennie. (Photo by Cecilia Nasmith, *Cobourg Daily Star*)

Her most characteristic work is highly detailed portraits of plants and animals in transparent watercolour or ink, directly from nature. Almost all the pictures in this book come from her journal pages: "My first journals were detailed records of all my natural history observations, both informed and naive, written in ruled volumes, and illustrated only occasionally with ink sketches. But through the years the journals seemed to set their own standards, and to demand ever more illustration. Each time as I portray a bit of the natural world I am again amazed at the gradual way in which its form and beauty come to notice. My responsibility for the truth of the image teaches me so much more than any less reconstructive methods of observation could.

I have found that to draw is to learn, and so intend to keep on learning."

In 1975 Aleta Karstad began watercolour portraits for Francis Cook's *Natural History of Canadian Amphibians and Reptiles*. This series continues to this day as living specimens of the rarer species are found.

In the spring of that year she set out with her husband, herpetologist Frederick W. Schueler, and friend Franklin D. Ross on coast-to-coast field work for *Canadian Nature Notebook*, an illustrated account of 25 common habitats. Other publications by Aleta Karstad and Fred Schueler include *Wild Seasons Daybook*, *North Moresby Wilderness: The Cumshewa Head Trail*, *Nature Walks in the Okanagan: A Guide to Three Trails* (co-authored with her father, Lars Karstad), and the forthcoming *This Fragile Inheritance: A Painter's Ecology of Glaciated North America*.